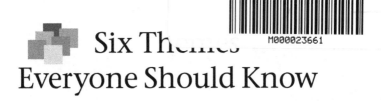

Six Themes
Everyone Should Know

Matthew

James E. Davison

Geneva
Press

© 2019 Geneva Press

First edition
Published by Geneva Press
Louisville, Kentucky

19 20 21 22 23 24 25 26 27 28—10 9 8 7 6 5 4 3 2 1

Unless otherwise indicated, Scripture quotations are from the New Revised Standard Version of the Bible, © 1989 by the Division of Christian Education of the National Council of the Churches of Christ in the U.S.A., and used by permission. In some instances, adaptations have been made to a Scripture or a confession to make the language inclusive.

Excerpts from the *Book of Order* and *Book of Confessions* have been used throughout this resource. Both are reprinted with permission of the Office of the General Assembly.

Cover designer: Rebecca Kueber

Library of Congress Cataloging-in-Publication Data

Names: Davison, James E., 1944- author.
Title: Six themes in Matthew everyone should know / James E. Davison.
Description: First [edition]. | Louisville, KY: Geneva Press, 2019. |
  Series: Six themes everyone should know series
Identifiers: LCCN 2018036030 (print) | LCCN 2018052649 (ebook) | ISBN
  9781611649222 (ebook) | ISBN 9781571532350 (pbk.)
Subjects: LCSH: Bible. Matthew--Theology--Textbooks.
Classification: LCC BS2575.52 (ebook) | LCC BS2575.52 .D38 2019 (print) |
  DDC 226.2/06--dc23
LC record available at https://lccn.loc.gov/2018036030

Contents

Six Themes Everyone Should Know series

The Bible, by Barry Ensign-George

Genesis, by W. Eugene March

Matthew, by James E. Davison

Luke, by John T. Carroll

1 and 2 Timothy, by Thomas G. Long

Introduction to the
Six Themes Everyone Should Know series

The *Six Themes Everyone Should Know* series focuses on the study of Scripture. Bible study is vital to the lives of churches. Churches need ways of studying Scripture that can fit a variety of contexts and group needs. *Six Themes Everyone Should Know* studies offer a central feature of church adult educational programs. Their flexibility and accessibility make it possible to have short-term studies that introduce biblical books and their main themes.

Six Themes Everyone Should Know consists of six chapters that introduce major biblical themes. At the core of each chapter is an introduction and three major sections. These sections relate to key dimensions of Bible study. These sections ask:
- What does this biblical theme mean?
- What is the meaning of this biblical theme for the life of faith?
- What does this biblical theme mean for the church at this point in history for action?

This format presents a compact and accessible way for people in various educational settings to gain knowledge about major themes in the biblical books; to experience the impact of what Scripture means for Christian devotion to God; and to consider ways Scripture can lead to new directions for the church in action.

Introduction to *Matthew*

The Gospel according to Matthew is the first book of the New Testament and the first of the four Gospels. Along with the evangelists Mark, Luke, and John, Matthew provides an account of the life and ministries of Jesus. Matthew begins with the genealogy (1:1–17) and birth of Jesus (1:18–25) and ends with Jesus' commissioning his disciples, after his resurrection, to "make disciples of all nations" and his promise: "I am with you always, to the end of the age" (28:16–20).

The church has always found Matthew's Gospel to be a rich source for understanding who Jesus of Nazareth was and what he said and did. This study looks at the main themes in Matthew's Gospel. It focuses on Jesus as Messiah as a beginning point for considering Matthew's perspective of who his Gospel is about as it portrays the life and ministry of Jesus Christ. Jesus' important teachings are explored, and we find how they shape our Christian lives today. They give the church—as the community of faith—directions for its mission and ministries in the world. These focuses strengthen our faith. They nourish our lives even as we are challenged to be faithful disciples of Jesus Christ and to embody his teachings in our daily living. Matthew's Gospel can be a vital source of renewal for the church's life and our own Christian experience as we seek to follow Jesus in word and deed.

John Calvin wrote that Matthew, as one of the four evangelists, sets before our eyes "Christ, sent by the Father, that our faith may recognize in Him the Author of the life of blessedness."[1]

May our lives be blessed by this study of the Gospel according to Matthew.

---

1. John Calvin, *A Harmony of the Gospels Matthew, Mark and Luke*, ed. David W. Torrance and Thomas F. Torrance, trans. A. W. Morrison, Calvin's New Testament Commentaries, 12 vols. (1972; repr., Grand Rapids: Wm. B. Eerdmans Publishing Co., 1995), xii.

Biblical Backgrounds to Matthew

Author and Date
The Gospel according to Matthew was "most likely written about A.D. 90 by an unknown Christian who was most probably at home in a church located in or near Antioch of Syria. The date of A.D. 90 commends itself because the destruction of Jerusalem appears to be an event that was rapidly receding into the past [22:7]."
—Jack Dean Kingsbury, "Matthew, the Gospel according to,"
in *Harper's Bible Dictionary*, ed. Paul J. Achtemeier
(San Francisco: Harper & Row, Publishers, 1985), 613.

Composition
"For most scholars, the Two-Source Hypothesis still explains best the composition of Matthew. Apparently, the author drew on two written sources: Mark and a collection of sayings of Jesus called Q. In addition, he used traditions available only to him (M). From these, he fashioned a theologically sophisticated story of the life and ministry of Jesus. The formula at 4:17 and at 16:21 divides this story into three main parts: the figure of Jesus Messiah (1:1–4:16); the public ministry of Jesus Messiah and Israel's repudiation of him (4:17–16:20); and the journey of Jesus Messiah to Jerusalem and his suffering, death, and resurrection (16:21–28:20)."
—*Harper's Bible Dictionary*, 613–14.

Importance
One perspective on Matthew's importance is that "there are indications, such as the Greek word *biblos*, "book," in the title and the *five* major discourses in chapters 5–7, 10, 13, 18, and 24–25 that Matthew intended his work to serve as a foundation book for his community, like the Torah or five books of Moses in the synagogue. In fact, Matthew came to serve as a preeminent Gospel for the church as a whole. From the second century on, it is the most widely cited Gospel and the most frequently read in ancient liturgical lectionaries."
—Reginald H. Fuller, "Matthew" in *Harper's Bible Commentary*, ed.
James L. Mays (San Francisco: Harper & Row, Publishers, 1988), 951.

Jesus diverges from the usual expectation of Messiah in Israel, both in his own personal identity as the Son of God and Emmanuel and for his mission as one who serves and suffers for humanity.

Chapter 1

Embracing Jesus as Messiah

Scripture

The best way to begin a study of Matthew is to read the entire Gospel quickly. Do not look for details, but focus simply on getting a sense for the whole. You will begin to see patterns in Matthew's way of presenting Jesus' ministry, and you will also note words, phrases, and thoughts that recur frequently in the text.

Matthew 1:1, 17–25   describes the ancestry and birth of Jesus, including important names he is given.

Matthew 8:1–27   shows the great power Jesus possessed to heal those in need.

Matthew 11:25–12:14   portrays the deep compassion Jesus has for people and, in the process, makes clear his authority as the Son.

Matthew 25:31–46   narrates the important parable of the Sheep and the Goats, which we will refer to regularly in this study.

Prayer

Gracious God, who created the world and all in it, I praise your name for your marvelous works, for stars and planets, for seas and mountains, for us and all living creatures. That you created us in your very image is wonderful beyond words. In the face of our faults and failures, that you have sent your Son to redeem us is far more than we could ever imagine, much less deserve. At the beginning of this study, I ask that you grant me insight to understand Jesus' teachings more fully. Draw me closer to him, the Messiah, your own beloved Son. Amen.

Introduction

Nearly one thousand years elapsed from King David's time to the birth of Jesus. During most of that period, Israel suffered under the domination of foreign rulers. As successive occupying empires became increasingly powerful, any hope of relief grew progressively dimmer. Many began to hope for the Lord God to intervene directly to free the nation and restore Israel's kingdom. How God might accomplish this miraculous intervention became the subject for much speculation, and many concluded that God would send armies of angelic beings to rescue the nation. Many also expected that a warrior king—a "messiah"—would lead these heavenly hosts.

Messiah is the Hebrew term for "anointed one," a reference to the fact that kings were anointed with oil as part of coronation ceremonies. Our word "Christ" derives from the equivalent Greek term for this symbolic act. Not surprisingly, hopes for a messiah often identified him with David—Israel's early, great ruler—hailing him as the "Son of David." As a mighty leader, the Messiah would guide Israel to victory over all the surrounding nations.

As we know, Jesus did not fit such a portrait at all. Born to a carpenter's family in poverty and a controversial itinerant preacher by trade, he was condemned to a despised death. Thus, in this Gospel, Matthew sets out to show that despite all outward appearances, Jesus is indeed Israel's expected Messiah. Not only that, Matthew asserts, Jesus as Messiah is much more than Israel could have anticipated.

While Matthew stands first in the New Testament, the Gospel of Mark was probably written earlier. Matthew appears to follow Mark's outline, adding a broad range of Jesus' teachings to Mark's many stories of Jesus' marvelous deeds. Matthew also adds further material, like the beautiful Christmas stories, editing all his material carefully. The end result is a well-rounded portrayal of Jesus' entire earthly life, all aimed at substantiating faith in Jesus as the true Messiah.

Matthew is traditionally identified as one of the twelve disciples, a tax collector by trade. For a variety reasons, most scholars believe that in fact the author is unknown, but he probably was connected with the disciple. For our purposes, it is sufficient to refer to the writer as "Matthew."

A Basic Theme: What Sort of Messiah Is Jesus?

Matthew describes the beginning of Jesus' public ministry in this way: "Jesus went throughout Galilee, teaching in their synagogues and proclaiming the good news of the kingdom, and curing every disease and every sickness among the people" (4:23). With this summary description, Matthew makes clear that Jesus the Messiah possesses marvelous divine power as he conducts his ministry.

Throughout the Gospel, Matthew narrates healings of individuals who suffer from illnesses or other physical disorders. Oftentimes, the healings occur among large crowds gathered around Jesus. At other times, a cure occurs more privately, as when Jesus enters Peter's home and heals his mother-in-law (8:14). The power of Jesus to heal is so great, in fact, that he simply tells a centurion that his servant, who is lying paralyzed in the centurion's home, will be healed, "and the servant was healed in that hour" (8:13).

As awe-inspiring as such physical healings may be, they are surpassed by other marvelous events through which Jesus demonstrates authority even over natural phenomena. He stills a storm on the Sea of Galilee (8:23–27) and later walks on its waters (14:22–33). He feeds more than five thousand people miraculously (14:13–21). Later, Jesus repeats this marvel with a crowd of over four thousand (15:32–39).

But there is another side to Matthew's portrait of Jesus as the Messiah: he acts as a servant of others. The disciples must have been shocked when Jesus informed them they were not to be like rulers who "lord it over" others, but instead to serve, as he himself does: "The Son of Man came not to be served but to serve, and to give his life a ransom for many" (20:28). The last phrase specifies what lengths Jesus is willing to go to aid others. This Messiah will *die* to bring redemption to humanity.

It should not be surprising that this Son of David differs greatly from Israel's expectation. But further, Matthew stresses not only that Jesus is the Messiah but that he is also the Son of God. While the Gospel is clear about the fact that Jesus is fully a human being, Matthew also puts emphasis on his divine nature. At Jesus' baptism, a voice from heaven proclaims, "This is my Son, the Beloved, with whom I am well pleased" (3:17). Later in the Gospel, various people call Jesus God's Son, including the disciples, Peter, and finally the Roman centurion at the cross (27:54).

In summary, Matthew wants us to recognize in Jesus the long-hoped for Messiah, but one who will do much more than reign over Israel and the world. Jesus also brings redemption from human weaknesses and failures, as he sacrifices himself by dying on behalf of humanity and thus offering forgiveness of sins. This is the point of Jesus' words as he offers the cup at the Last Supper: "This is my blood of the covenant, which is poured out for many for the forgiveness of sins" (26:28). Ultimately, Matthew affirms that the words of the prophet Isaiah point to Jesus' true identity as Messiah: "His name shall be called Emmanuel" (1:23; RSV).

The Life of Faith: Trust in the Lord of Life

In answer to a question about the greatest commandment, Jesus quotes Deuteronomy 6:5: "'You shall love the Lord your God with all your heart, and with all your soul, and with all your mind'" (22:37). The answer is not surprising, because all Jews recognized this as their central affirmation of faith. The real surprise comes in Matthew's repeated emphasis that Jesus, as the Son of God, deserves the same honor as does God. Jesus' words in the Great Commission at the end of the Gospel confirm this: "All authority in heaven and on earth has been given to me" (28:18). Then he instructs his followers to baptize "in the name of the Father, and of the Son and of the Holy Spirit." This early Trinitarian formula makes it quite clear that faithfulness to God entails trusting in Jesus too.

Practically speaking, this means that not just the Father but Jesus too deserves worship and honor. Notice the parable of the Sheep and the Goats: "When the Son of Man comes in his glory, and all the angels with him, then he will sit on the throne of his glory" (25:31). When Matthew speaks of people in authoritative positions, he often pictures them as "sitting." The image recalls kings seated on thrones with petitioners standing or kneeling before them. Thus, Matthew notes that, when Jesus delivers the Sermon on the Mount, he "sits down" (5:1). Further, we read that at the end of the age, "the Son of Man [will be] seated at the right hand of Power and coming on the clouds of heaven" (26:64).

Matthew also emphasizes that we turn to Jesus as Messiah for forgiveness of sins. Then as now, people assumed only God can forgive sins. Yet Jesus claims that same power. In chapter 9:2–7, as he heals a paralyzed man, he says, "So that you may know that the Son of Man has authority on earth to forgive sins." Now, as Matthew emphasizes, Jesus not only forgives sins but brings about the possibility of forgiveness by his death. In Joseph's dream at the beginning of the Gospel, the angel's instructions are to "name him Jesus [e.g., "God saves"], for he will save his people from their sins" (1:21). Then, near the end of the Gospel, at the final Passover supper, Jesus explains how this will happen: his blood would be "poured out for many for the forgiveness of sins" (26:28).

Throughout the Gospel, Matthew stresses that trusting in Jesus offers comfort and security in an uncertain world. Noting the fragility of life, Jesus tells his hearers not to be anxious about food or clothing, concluding, "Do not worry about tomorrow, for tomorrow will bring worries of its own" (6:34). Later, more personally, Jesus offers an invitation to take refuge in him: "Come to me, all you that are weary and are carrying heavy burdens, and I will give you rest" (11:28–29). Ultimately, this promise is valid because of what Matthew emphasizes both at the beginning and end of this Gospel: Jesus is "Emmanuel," and he "will be with us always." These statements serve as bookends to this Gospel, and they summarize Matthew's main message: Jesus, the Messiah, the Son of God, is with us always.

The Church: Confessing the Messiah in Current Culture
Faced with a trick question about Roman authority over God's chosen people, Jesus responds with the well-known words, "Render to Caesar the things that are Caesar's; and to God the things that are God's" (22:21; NASB). This Gospel, with other New Testament writings, does not question obedience to proper authorities. Still, Jesus' subtle response challenges any human claim—even an emperor's—to ultimate authority. God's Messiah, Matthew

stresses, is the true king. Jesus affirms that "the Son of Man is to come with his angels in the glory of his Father, and then he will repay everyone for what has been done" (16:27).

While this emphasis on supreme divine authority points most directly at dictators and autocrats, in our day it may also apply to an opposite tendency. Western culture emphasizes individualism to such a degree that it causes many to distrust any authority at all. Some common phrases in this view of things are: "All truth is relative," or "Institutions cannot be trusted," or "I'll do it my way." Obviously, the fact that the church has an institutional side makes it suspect in this environment. Unfortunately, misuse of authority in the church has too often given credence to doubt and suspicion.

Still, this Gospel proclaims that, in spite of failings in the church, there is such a thing as appropriate authority in our world. However, this authority does not reside in either human institutions or individuals. Rather, ultimate authority is found in God alone and in God's Son, Jesus the Messiah. Facing such conflicting views about authority in our day, the church needs to adopt ways to proclaim allegiance to God, without—at the same time—appearing to be autocratic itself.

But then there is a further question: Is Jesus really who this Gospel claims? The religious authorities in Jesus' day already asserted Jesus was a false teacher. Matthew was aware of a variety of accusations leveled at Jesus, and he sought to counter such denials at several points in this Gospel. His many statements that Jesus fulfills prophecies in the Scriptures provide indirect responses to these allegations. More explicitly, Matthew presents Joseph's dream to indicate that Jesus' birth is legitimate (1:20–22). Later, he notes that both Pilate and his wife, who has had a frightening dream, proclaim Jesus' innocence (27:18–24). Then, when Jesus hangs dead on the cross, a Roman centurion adds his confirmation: "Truly this man was God's Son!" (27:54). And finally, with a hint of mockery, Matthew reminds his readers of the unlikely story put out by the religious leaders after the resurrection, alleging that the disciples had stolen Jesus' body—even though the tomb was under guard (28:12–15).

Today, the popular position for many is that, far from being the Messiah, Jesus is simply one among several important religious figures. This Gospel answers that assessment with the clear proclamation that Jesus, while very human, is himself also divine. He is Emmanuel, "God with us." He is the Son of God. He is the One who "possesses all authority in heaven and on earth." In consequence, for Matthew all who believe in and worship the Lord God, at least implicitly, also believe in and worship Jesus.

For Reflection and Action

1. The Eastern Orthodox Churches traditionally put particular emphasis on the "Jesus Prayer." The full version reads: "Lord Jesus Christ, Son of God, have mercy on me a sinner." Think about how these words fit with the emphases in Matthew's Gospel. For the next week or so, try praying the prayer. Do they help to enrich your own spiritual life? *Matthew makes clear that Jesus, the Messiah, possesses divine power as he conducts his ministry and that he is Son of God. He will be w/us always*

2. What difference does it make to you if you think of the title "Jesus Messiah" in place of "Jesus Christ"? *Jesus Christ brings redemption from human weaknesses & failures. Sacrifices himself by dying on cross and offering forgiveness of sins. We can trust him to be w/us always*

3. In ancient Israel, people connected closeness to God with the temple in Jerusalem. What do you think Jesus means when he says, "Something greater than the temple is here" (12:6)? How does this statement relate to your own understanding of and trust in Jesus? *Deeds & miracles can be performed in places other than the Church/temple. Religion should be shown everywhere — He is w/us always.*

4. Matthew applies several titles to Jesus as the Messiah, such as "Son of David," "Son of Man," and "Son of God." How do you understand each of these, and do any of them speak to you specially? *That Jesus deserves same honor as God; that Jesus claims same power to forgive sins & that trusting Jesus offers comfort and security. Jesus is always w/us. all inspiring Son of God*

Jesus affirms the future coming of the kingdom of heaven and the nearness, or presence, of the kingdom already on the earth.

Chapter 2

Seeking the Kingdom of Heaven

Scripture

Matthew 3:1–4:25 relates the first events in Jesus' public life, as he is baptized by John, tempted by the devil, chooses his first disciples, and begins his ministry.

Matthew 11:1–19 discusses John the Baptist's prophetic ministry, along with the way in which Jesus conducts his own ministry.

Matthew 13:1–52 presents several "parables of the kingdom," which seek to explain some of the mystery about how God's kingdom operates on this earth.

Matthew 24:3–25:30 employs striking images to describe the time of the end, followed by parables that encourage preparation because that time will come unexpectedly.

Similar to the Lords' Prayer

Prayer

God Most High, I give thanks to you and praise your name as the Ruler of heaven and earth. All angels and archangels and the hosts who dwell in heaven live in peace, rejoicing in your goodness and delighting in your love and mercies. Here on earth, however, nation wars against nation, and people seek power over one another. Through the power of Jesus, the Messiah, I pray that you will cause your kingdom to come on this earth as it is in heaven.

Let humility reign, and grant that all of us may serve one another. In the name of Jesus, I pray. Amen.

Introduction

The reigns of David and Solomon, nearly one thousand years before the coming of Jesus, marked the golden age of the kingdom of the Jews. Trade increased, territory expanded, and Jerusalem prospered. Only two centuries later, however, the Assyrian Empire annexed the larger, northern section of the original kingdom. For the next 130 years, rulers in Judah presided over a small territory around Jerusalem. Kings in name only, they served as vassals under the major empires in the ancient Middle East. Then, with the destruction of Jerusalem and the resulting Babylonian Captivity in 586 B.C., the territory was turned into a province. For the next six centuries, the Jews remained subservient to whichever empire held sway at the time.

As noted in the first chapter, Jewish expectations for a renewed earthly kingdom gradually faded, to be replaced for many by the hope that God would intervene, perhaps by sending a messianic figure to lead the people out of bondage. Along with Jesus' role as God's Messiah, Matthew emphasizes the coming of God's kingdom. Early on, he reports that the "wise men" come to King Herod, asking, "Where is the child who has been born king of the Jews?" (2:2). In the next chapter, he introduces John the Baptist, who heralds the coming of Jesus with the message, "Repent, for the kingdom of heaven has come near" (3:2). Then, in chapter 4, Matthew portrays Jesus using these very same words to inaugurate his own ministry (4:17).

You may notice that, while the other Gospels speak of the "kingdom of God," Matthew almost always uses the phrase "kingdom of heaven." This preference is one of the most obvious examples of the fact that the Gospel is imbued with Jewish thought patterns and practices. So much is this the case that nearly all scholars agree that the author of Matthew was Jewish, although probably living outside Palestine, perhaps in a city like Antioch in Syria. Clearly, he was directing his Gospel toward a primarily Jewish audience. Consequently, since traditional Jewish practice avoided use of the name "God," Matthew employs a circumlocution, "heaven" instead.

A final note is in order here: the Greek term "kingdom" carries a more active connotation than it does in English, putting the stress more on the king's governing than on his territory. To underscore this point, translators sometimes use "reign of God (or heaven)" when interpreting this phrase.

A Basic Theme: What Sort of Kingdom Is This?

If Jesus is a much different Messiah than the Jews expected, then we can expect the kingdom he establishes will also be much different. It is not entirely different, of course, for the Jewish expectation is paralleled by Jesus' own regular references to a final, future kingdom. For instance, to a centurion in Capernaum, he says, "Many will come from east and west and will eat with Abraham and Isaac and Jacob in the kingdom of heaven" (8:11). Commenting on the threats to earthly possessions, Jesus cautions, "Store up for yourselves treasures in heaven, where neither moth nor rust consumes and where thieves do not break in and steal" (6:20).

As we noticed earlier, Matthew depicts Jesus speaking of his returning in glory frequently. Much Jewish conjecture about "the age to come" employed imagery depicting mighty signs in the heavens and brutal threats to God's people on earth as the Messiah comes to usher in the new age. These kinds of images, called "apocalyptic," are employed also by Jesus. Especially in chapter 24, he speaks in detail about signs that will usher in the new age, climaxing with his statement that all peoples "will see 'the Son of Man coming on the clouds of heaven' with power and great glory" (24:30).

At the same time, Matthew makes clear that the kingdom has already "come near" with the arrival of Jesus. But instead of a speedy sequence of astonishing signs ending with final judgment on the nations, Jesus travels around teaching, preaching, and healing. Even John the Baptist, who announced Jesus as the Messiah, begins to have doubts. He sends his own disciples to ask whether Jesus is really the One who is to come. The answer Jesus gives is, "Go and tell John what you hear and see: the blind receive their sight, the lame walk, the lepers are cleansed, the deaf hear, the dead are raised, and the poor have good news brought to them" (11:4–5). Jesus' response is indirect but telling, echoing language in the prophet Isaiah, who names these activities as the kinds of things that will occur when the future kingdom comes (Isaiah 29:18–19; 35:5–6).

In the following verses, Jesus talks somewhat cryptically about John, but the central point is an affirmation that John is indeed the forerunner who was prophesied to precede the Messiah. Jesus praises John, too, saying that "among those born of women no one has arisen greater than John the Baptist." Then he adds a qualifying comment: "Yet the least in the kingdom of heaven is greater than he" (11:11). In other words, John prepares the way for the kingdom to come, but with Jesus it has now arrived.

Thus, the kingdom of heaven encompasses both an "already" and a "not yet." While the final fullness will be unveiled in the future, the seeds of the kingdom are already present and active in the world. Those seeds appear first in Jesus' own ministry, but they come to expression also in the actions of "sons and daughters of the kingdom" who "seek first God's kingdom and his righteousness" (6:33), who "forgive others their trespasses" (6:14), who show mercy towards others (9:13), and who do "the will of my Father in heaven" (7:21).

The Life of Faith: Desiring the Kingdom

Throughout Christian history, people have tried to calculate the time when Christ will return in glory. Many today continue to speculate about these matters, although in Matthew—in Jesus' depiction of apocalyptic events at the end of the age—he himself remarks that "about that day and hour no one knows, neither the angels of heaven, *nor the Son*, but only the Father" (24:36). A few sentences later, he cautions the disciples to "keep awake therefore, for you do not know on what day your Lord is coming" (24:42). Then, in a parable about ten bridesmaids, Jesus repeats this admonition again, "Keep awake therefore, for you know neither the day nor the hour" (25:13).

However, that Jesus will return at an unexpected time does not take away from the fact that believers in him can long for—indeed, *pray* for—the coming of the final kingdom. In fact, that is precisely what Christians pray regularly in most worship services around the globe, "*Your kingdom come. Your will be done, on earth as it is in heaven*" (6:10). Further, several of Jesus' statements in Matthew urge believers in him to ready themselves for his return.

We have already seen this in the previous paragraph, where Jesus cautions listeners to "keep awake!" In another parable, Jesus compares a faithful slave to a wicked one, where the latter tries to take advantage of his master's delayed return. The master will arrive unexpectedly, Jesus warns, and will judge the wicked slave for his unfaithful service (24:45–51).

Early Christians naturally assumed that Jesus' "second coming" would be speedy. Perhaps two thousand years later, we cannot feel the same sense of urgency that our predecessors did, but these admonitions to steadfastness and faithfulness remain relevant nonetheless. Additionally, Matthew encourages believers to look for signs of the kingdom. More often than not, those signs will be small and easy to overlook. In the parable of the Mustard Seed, Jesus chooses the smallest seed known at the time, indicating that "when it has grown it is the greatest of shrubs and becomes a tree, so that the birds of the air come and make nests in its branches" (13:31–32). His parable of the Yeast makes a similar point: "The kingdom of heaven is like yeast that a woman took and mixed with three measures of flour until all of it was leavened" (13:33).

The kingdom may come quietly, but its great significance leads to Jesus' familiar words encouraging the disciples to "strive first for the kingdom of God and his righteousness" (6:33). Later in the Gospel, two brief parables of Jesus stress this point. In one, a man uncovers a great treasure in a field. He promptly buys the field and takes possession of his find. Likewise, in the following parable, a merchant, finding a pearl of great value, sells everything else in order to possess it (13:44–46). While the point is obvious, it is an easy one for the disciples, and us, to forget: the kingdom of the Father is the most valuable possession anyone can gain.

The reason is clear: the Father, Jesus proclaims, "gives good things" (7:11), and the Father "knows what you need before you ask him" (6:8). The greatest gift, Matthew stresses, is Jesus himself, who gives his life "a ransom for many" (20:28). The Messiah, in other words, even at the cost of his life, wishes to embrace us with open arms and draw us into the kingdom.

The Church: Whose Kingdom Does the Church Promote?

Immediately after recording John's baptism of Jesus, Matthew—again following Mark's outline—describes the temptations of

Jesus in the wilderness. The three specific temptations depicted in Matthew culminate as the tempter takes Jesus to a "very high mountain" and promises "all the kingdoms of the world and their splendor" to Jesus in return for his allegiance (4:8–9). Notice how subtle this temptation is. Mountains often symbolized closeness to God and divine revelation. Thus, Matthew situates the "Sermon on the Mount" on a mountain, and the Transfiguration later in the Gospel occurs on a "high mountain" (17:1). The tempter, then, pretends to enjoy divine authority when he makes this final offer, but Jesus recognizes the deception and quotes Scripture in reply: "Worship the Lord your God, and serve only him" (4:10).

Ultimately, all the kingdoms in the world are subject to the Lord God alone, and all the rulers of these kingdoms ought to offer their primary allegiance to the one ultimate rule, the kingdom of heaven. As we know, however, this has never come to fruition. Every society, nation, or kingdom tends over time to build itself around power and hold onto that power. This is the precise opposite of "strive first for the kingdom of God" (6:33). And it is diametrically opposed to Jesus' response when the disciples ask him the misguided question, "Who is the greatest in the kingdom of heaven?" Pointing to a child, Jesus proclaims that "whoever becomes humble like this child is the greatest in the kingdom of heaven" (18:1–4).

However, humility has been in short supply for most nations and rulers, as Israel's own history also indicates. The Hebrew Scriptures warn the people regularly about the ever-present danger of pride because of their status as God's special people. Thus, early in Matthew's Gospel, when Jewish leaders come to John the Baptist, he scolds them for their presumption in being children of Abraham: "For I tell you, God is able from these stones to raise up children to Abraham" (3:9).

The message of the kingdom of heaven in Matthew, thus, means that no kingdom, or nation, or people, should consider itself above all others. There is no hint here that only some nations are special, and none can boast that their nation is better than others, much less the best or God's special favorite. After all, God's original promise to Abraham contained the declaration that "in you all the families of the earth shall be blessed" (Genesis 12:3).

Now, in Matthew, as Jesus completes his earthly mission, his final words of commission to the disciples are, "Go therefore and make disciples of *all nations*" (28:19).

For the church today, this implies that Christians must avoid claims and attitudes, in ourselves as well as others, that one particular nation is more special in God's eyes than others. The same applies regarding our approach to "church." When Matthew refers to the church, the word refers to the community or assembly of believers, not directly to an institution as such. Any institution, including the church and our many denominational groupings, can take on a life of its own, forgetting that its only purpose is to be an instrument that the Spirit can use to help bring the kingdom of heaven more completely to fulfillment.

For Reflection and Action

1. In the Lord's Prayer, we are encouraged to pray for the kingdom to come. During the next week, focus on this petition and reflect on special ways the kingdom could be present more fully here and now so that our world and lives are more like the kingdom when it arrives fully in the future. *Be more humble and serve one another.*

2. In practical terms, what does it mean for you to follow Jesus' instruction in the Sermon on the Mount to "seek first the kingdom of God"? *Forgive others their trespasses, show mercy toward others and do the will of the Father in Heaven*

3. The Gospel of Matthew teaches that, even though the kingdom of heaven has not yet come in fullness, it has already been inaugurated in the coming of Jesus the Messiah. Where might you see, or have you seen, signs of the presence of the kingdom in your life or in the world around you? *See List Pg. 57 thru people of faith, nurses/doctors/teachers (especially during Covid-19)*

4. What is it, do you think, in nations and denominations that leads to boasting about being special or better than others? How can we counter that attitude, also in ourselves, perhaps? *Be more humble, Respect the views and beliefs of others. No one is above others Belong to God alone.*

(over)

Sow our seeds thru

1) Prayer
2) Read Bible
3) Worship services
4) Repentance
4) Familiarize Bible Verses
5) Praise
6) Be Thankful

*Consider the subtleties of evil. Structural evil in
society is usually hidden unless it is pointed out to us.
The evil in our own hearts is so easy to overlook, deny,
or simply not recognize.*

Chapter 3

Fleeing Evil

Scripture

Matthew 2:1–23   narrates the story of the wise men, who come to worship the baby Jesus, and the reaction of the powerful, but despised, king Herod, who wants to destroy him.

Matthew 5:1–48   contains the first chapter of the "Sermon on the Mount," in which Matthew provides a detailed summary of Jesus' teachings, including his famous "Beatitudes" that introduce the sermon.

Matthew 7:1–12   comes from the last chapter of the Sermon on the Mount and emphasizes Jesus' teachings about the importance of our attitudes and actions toward others.

Prayer

Righteous and gracious God, you have called all people to live according to your will, but we have often chosen evil paths, falling victim to temptations and treating others in ways that benefit us, often at their expense. We confess that we, too, have fallen far short of your will. Guard us from evil powers. Cleanse our heart so that what we say and do may match our thoughts and desires. By your Spirit, restrain the power of evil in the world, and enable us all, but especially those of us who bear the name of Jesus, to show his love to all. Amen.

Introduction

For ancient Israel, the word "evil" covered a broad range of troubles, including disasters, misfortune, and illness. More often, as you would expect, it pointed to human moral failures. The philosophical question of how evil originated was of little interest to the Israelites. Mostly, they appear to have been content to maintain that the first human beings, Adam and Eve, disobeyed God's command and that everyone since then has continued to fall into sin. The story of the Garden of Eden in Genesis 1 does picture a tempter in the form of a serpent, and Christian writers have usually identified the tempter with a personal evil being, Satan.

Later books of the Hebrew Scriptures themselves, however, contain only scattered references to Satan. In fact, in the book of Job, which speaks most clearly of Satan, he is portrayed as a servant, not an opponent, of God. The biblical authors, in other words, usually speak of evil, along with everything else in the creation, as under God's ultimate control.

By the time of Jesus, however, Israel's picture of the evil one had changed radically. It had become commonplace to visualize an evil dominion headed by Satan and embracing a host of evil spirits, or demons. This "kingdom of Satan" was understood to resist the kingdom of heaven wherever possible by inciting humans into all manner of sinful actions. Rulers, like emperors and kings, were obvious targets of the evil powers because of the great evil they could provoke in their realms. Matthew offers an obvious example in the Gospel, when he relates the story of Herod the Great's orders to his soldiers to kill all the baby boys up to the age of two in the environs of Bethlehem (2:16, CEV).

The Hebrew Scriptures concentrate particularly on the evil thoughts and deeds the servants of Satan can inflame in human hearts. It is this sort of evil, too, that Matthew is especially concerned with: the actions of individual men and women that dishonor God and harm other human beings. As you read the Gospel, notice how Matthew describes evil with a variety of terms. In addition to the word "sin," you will encounter terms like "unrighteousness," "lawlessness," and "evildoing."

A Basic Theme: Why Is Evil a Problem for Humans?

As we have observed, evil appears already in the opening stories of the Gospel of Matthew in Herod's attempt to murder the baby

Jesus. Then, after a brief description of Jesus' baptism, Matthew introduces the devil, or Satan, who tempts Jesus for forty days and nights in the wilderness (4:1–11). By relaying these stories early in the Gospel, Matthew emphasizes how frightening the power of evil is. If Jesus himself can be threatened by the dominion of Satan, then all God's children are at great risk of destruction. There is good reason for the Lord's Prayer to include the petition, "And lead us not into temptation, but deliver us from evil [or 'the evil one']" (6:13; KJV).

It might seem that, since the kingdom of the Father is now present in the world, evil would no longer represent such a danger. However, remember the "not yet" we spoke of regarding the kingdom. Because final fulfillment remains in the future, the destructive power of evil continues to affect human lives and society. Chapter 13 of Matthew contains several parables that speak to this continuing threat to humanity. In the parable of the Sower, Jesus describes four ways that seed, meaning "the word of the kingdom," can land on the soil. With reference to seed falling along the path, Jesus explains that "when anyone hears the word of the kingdom and does not understand it, the evil one comes and snatches away what is sown in the heart" (13:19).

More ominously, the following parable pictures a field that has been planted with good seed. At night, "an enemy came and sowed weeds among the wheat." The sower decides not to replant but to wait for the harvest, when he will gather the grain but burn the weeds (13:24–30). When the disciples ask Jesus to explain the parable, he identifies the sower as the Son of Man, the enemy as the devil, the good seed as the "children of the kingdom," and the weeds as the "children of the evil one" (13:36–41).

Now of course this parable implies that there will come a time when evil will no longer threaten God's kingdom. At the "end of the age," Jesus proclaims, "the Son of Man will send his angels, and they will collect out of his kingdom all causes of sin and all evildoers" (13:40–41). Then, in a parable about casting a net into the sea, Jesus makes the same point: when the fishermen retrieve the net, they will separate the good from the evil catch (13:47–50). By relating these parables, Matthew affirms the general teaching found throughout the New Testament of a final reckoning with sin and evil when "the righteous will shine like the sun in the kingdom of their Father" (13:43).

While these parables might give the impression that humans are simply pawns in the hands of the Father or the devil, the continuous appeals throughout Matthew to repent, to believe, to listen, and the like, indicate that humans retain responsibility to live in a manner that fits them for the Father's kingdom. We can best demonstrate this conclusion by remembering the parable of the Sheep and the Goats, where Jesus emphasizes that the actions of human beings—for good or bad—determine which group they belong to and whose kingdom they serve (25:31–46).

The Life of Faith: How Do We Deal with Evil?

These descriptions of judgment at the end of the age highlight in stark tones just how seriously God takes human choices and actions. Other words of Jesus in Matthew, too, may well have struck fear in the hearts of the disciples and the crowds. Think of this comment, "I tell you, on the day of judgment you will have to give an account for every careless word you utter" (12:36). Or consider this warning: "Unless your righteousness exceeds that of the scribes and Pharisees, you will never enter the kingdom of heaven" (5:20).

Knowing how weak we often are, and how far we may fall short of consistently doing the will of the Father, we may also experience the anxiety that probably plagued the disciples. However, these warnings go hand in hand with positive words of Jesus depicting how believers in him should think, speak, and live. We will look at this in more detail in the next chapter. Here, consider the underlying issue Matthew raises regularly throughout the Gospel.

In the Sermon on the Mount, immediately following the requirement to display greater righteousness than that of the Pharisees and scribes, Jesus offers a series of examples of how disciples ought to treat others. They must avoid not only murder but also anger. They must abstain not only from adultery but also from lust. They must love not only neighbors but also enemies. All these examples locate inner motives as the source of true righteousness (5:21–48). Later, Jesus makes this point sharply when the Jewish leaders accuse him of violating the law: "You brood of vipers! How can you speak good things, when you are evil? For out of the abundance of the heart the mouth speaks" (12:34).

20   Matthew

avoid anger
abstain from lust
love — neighbors, and enemies

Later in Matthew, another controversy breaks out between Jesus and the religious leaders. The latter censure Jesus for allowing his disciples to eat without washing their hands, a ritual practice that was part of the tradition. Jesus counters with his own charge that the Pharisees have devised a tradition that allows them to violate one of the Ten Commandments, "Honor your father and your mother" (Exodus 20:12). Then Jesus asserts that what defiles people is not what they put into their mouths but what they say. In other words, this is a question of the heart. And so, in conclusion Jesus pronounces, "For out of the heart come evil intentions, murder, adultery, fornication, theft, false witness, slander" (15:19).

As these passages make clear, it is not just words and actions that matter; it is also the thoughts and motives of the heart. In the Sermon on the Mount, Jesus explains his famous comment, "Do not judge, so that you may not be judged" by warning, "For with the judgment you make you will be judged." Then he adds a further caution, "Why do you see the speck in your neighbor's eye, but do not notice the log in your own eye?" (7:1–3). These comments imply a heart that is pure, like the sixth beatitude, "Blessed are the pure in heart, for they will see God" (5:8), and they offer practical examples of the "Golden Rule": "In everything do to others as you would have them do to you; for this is the law and the prophets" (7:12).

The Church: Responding to Evil in Human Society

In Jesus' day, the power of Satan and his kingdom of demons was an accepted explanation for the evil that people experienced in their everyday lives. While we may think differently today about how evil operates, we will not doubt the power of evil in this world and also in human hearts. These days, the term "structural evil" is used to designate the awareness that evil infects the very fabric of society. It is not just that some persons do evil, but the arrangement of political and social institutions itself can foster evil practices that harm individuals, usually the poorer, more vulnerable members of society.

Additionally, as evil rulers strive to gain or retain power, their actions often harm innocent bystanders. As we have seen, Matthew records an example of this sort of "collateral damage." In order to kill one baby, Herod orders his troops to destroy all the infant boys in Bethlehem under the age of two. The lament that he quotes from Jeremiah has been echoed down through history: "A voice was heard in Ramah, wailing and loud lamentation, Rachel weeping for her children" (2:18).

While evil rulers may not care about the harm they inflict on others, Jesus counsels a different way. Throughout Matthew, we find Jesus admonishing the disciples to respect children (19:13–15); urging sympathy for the common folk, who are "harassed and helpless, like sheep without a shepherd" (9:36); advocating aid for "the least of these" (25:40); and appealing to those who are "weary and are carrying heavy burdens" to come to him for comfort (11:28). It is worth noting that what Jesus called for was not new. It follows the lead of the Hebrew Scriptures, where both the Law and the Prophets issue regular demands for compassionate treatment of the vulnerable members of society, especially widows, orphans, the poor, and aliens.

Unfortunately, autocratic rulers—in Israel as well as elsewhere—have usually not been inclined to focus on compassion and mercy, much less justice. Nevertheless, Jesus' words and example have compelled believers in him to act differently, whether or not they could have any effect on the structures of society as a whole. Living in Western democracies, the church today is able to exert influence in society and to foster justice, compassion, and peace. The challenge, naturally, is that believers in Jesus often do not agree on what political and social structures best promote these ideals. The further challenge is to follow the two sides of Jesus' teaching that we have seen repeatedly in Matthew—his call to maintain a high standard of righteousness and his appeal for mercy and compassion. Thus, the issue becomes one of striving to recognize the appropriate response in differing situations. For instance: When is mercy simply leniency? When is justice really severity?

Answers to such questions are not easy, but communities of believers in Jesus are obliged to deal with the issues and to witness to the values of the kingdom of heaven. In the process, we should bear in mind that the command of Jesus to love all people also applies to us as his disciples, whatever our denomination, political persuasion, or racial-ethnic or social group may be.

For Reflection and Action

1. "Fleeing evil" sounds straightforward enough, but in practice it is difficult, and sometimes it can be extremely difficult even to recognize the threat when it comes. Reflect on ways you may be threatened by evil. How might you recognize the dangers so that you can hold fast to the Messiah? *not respecting peaceful protests, holding grudges, showing mercy and compassion to less fortunate.*

2. What does the title of this chapter "Fleeing Evil" mean to you, and how might it relate to the petition in the Lord's Prayer, "Lead us not into temptation, but deliver us from evil"? *actions of humans can dishonor God and harm other humans. Emphasizes how frightening the power of evil is. On day of judgment, you will have to account for every careless word you utter*

3. Jesus warns against "judging others." Why is judging so tempting, and how might the practice of judging others be connected to the attitude of our hearts? *Not just words + actions, but also our thoughts and motives of the heart. Do not judge, so that you may not be judged*

4. What do you understand by the expression "structural evil"? Do you see any persons or groups who are impacted by it, and what do you think disciples of Jesus can or should do about it?

awareness that evil infects the very fabric of society. Not just people do evil — political and social institutions can foster evil practices.

usually, the poor + more vulnerable.

Jesus teachings - respect children, sympathy for the common folk harassed + helpless aid for the "least of these" weary and carrying heavy burdens to come to him for comfort

*Matthew seems to be writing to provide a kind of
"manual for discipleship." Along with righteousness,
one of his central themes is love.*

Chapter 4

Following Jesus

Scripture

Matthew 9:9–13; 10:1–4, 34–39   speak of Jesus' call to Matthew
and the other disciples, and record some of Jesus' comments about
the intent of his ministry.

Matthew 16:13–23   records Peter's great declaration about Jesus'
identity, followed by his failure to accept Jesus' teaching about the
crucifixion and resurrection to come.

Matthew 19:16–30   relates the interchange between the rich
young man and Jesus regarding the requirements for entering the
kingdom.

Matthew 26:57–75   narrates the beginning of the trials that Jesus
faced before the authorities and Peter's three denials that he is a
disciple of Jesus.

Prayer

God of love, who calls us all to be followers of Jesus the Messiah,
that you wish us to be like those disciples whom Jesus called to
himself is a gift of your grace. We know that the way of discipleship can be hard and, for some, treacherous. Yet we know, too, that
your Son will always be with us. I thank you for your call to me also
to be a follower of Jesus. Uphold me when I fail, as the disciples

did. Grant me strength to live humbly, with mercy and love for all whom I meet. In Jesus' name. Amen.

Introduction

When John the Baptist appeared in the Judean wilderness with the message, "Repent, for the kingdom of heaven has come near," his strange dress and powerful message reminded many of the revered prophets of ancient Israel (3:1–6). Though the writings of the Hebrew Bible do not mention this often, it appears that the prophets gathered others around them who were sympathetic to their messages. The most famous of these was Baruch, who was close to the prophet Jeremiah (Jeremiah 36:1–8). Like the prophets, John the Baptist, too, had followers, as we learn when Matthew narrates a visit to Jesus by John's disciples (Matthew 11:1–6).

Because of Jesus' words and actions, some considered him to be a prophet also (21:11). Like the prophets of old, he, too, had disciples. Matthew says repeatedly that Jesus drew crowds of people—often "great crowds"—who followed him around. The twelve disciples, however, formed an inner core of followers, whom Jesus called specifically to join him (10:1–4). When Jesus found the first four—Peter, Andrew, James, and John—fishing by the Sea of Galilee, he called them with the words, "Follow me, and I will make you fish for people" (4:19). The person whose name is on this Gospel, the tax collector Matthew, heard the same call (9:9), and we can imagine that Jesus used similar words when he called the other eight. These twelve followed Jesus continually. As the official leaders of Jesus' movement, they came to be designated "the apostles" in the early church.

It is worth noting that the twelve were not the only ones who traveled with Jesus during his ministry. Several women were also followers, accompanying Jesus on his travels and helping to sustain his ministry. Matthew mentions them in the scene at the cross: "Many women were also there, looking on from a distance; they had followed Jesus from Galilee and had provided for him" (27:55).

The Gospel of Matthew is often called a "manual of discipleship." One of its purposes is to paint a portrait of what following Jesus the Messiah means. Thus, Matthew intends for the disciples to be seen as models, and he encourages his readers to emulate their successes and avoid their failures as they strive to be disciples too.

A Basic Theme: What It Means to "Follow Jesus" ✓

For Matthew, Jesus' words to the disciples, "Follow me," are also directed to all believers. Given the themes that we have already encountered—Jesus the Messiah, Son of David, and Son of God, the one who will destroy evil and be seated in glory in the kingdom of heaven—the primary calling for everyone is to place following him above any other commitment. Thus, Mark and Luke, along with Matthew, record this warning: "Whoever loves father or mother more than me is not worthy of me; and whoever loves son or daughter more than me is not worthy of me" (10:37).

Once, while Jesus is speaking with the crowds, someone tells him that his family has arrived. Jesus responds by pointing at his disciples, saying, "Here are my mother and my brothers! For whoever does the will of my Father in heaven is my brother and sister and mother" (12:46–49). These statements by Jesus, and others scattered throughout the Gospels, sometimes sound unnecessarily severe. Hyperbole, harsh words, and either-or language, however, were frequent features of preaching in the ancient world, and they functioned to emphasize the speaker's point. In this case, Jesus' strong language stresses the primary need for commitment to him and to God.

At the same time, Jesus also emphasizes the loving character of the heavenly Father, who gives "good gifts" to his children (7:11) and who sends the sun and the rain not only for good or righteous people but also for those who are not (5:45). Further, Jesus often speaks tenderly and compassionately, inviting the crowds to "come to me, all you that are weary and are carrying heavy burdens, and I will give you rest" (11:28). By presenting Jesus' severe words, then, Matthew does not intend to portray a stern Lord but to underline the urgency of living according to God's will.

The famous saying in the book of Proverbs, "Pride goes before destruction, and a haughty spirit before a fall" (Proverbs 16:18), captures the underlying issue here. From the story of the fall in Genesis onward, the Hebrew Scriptures repeatedly condemn pride and praise humility. The writers of the New Testament do the same. This should not be surprising when we recall that the attitude of our hearts is central to doing God's will. Thus, as Matthew depicts Jesus' ministry, he points to the necessity of humility in following the Messiah.

At one point in the Gospel, the disciples approach Jesus with the question, "Who is the greatest in the kingdom of heaven?" Jesus' almost matter-of-fact response is that "unless you change and become like children, you will never enter the kingdom of heaven." Then Jesus proclaims that "the greatest in the kingdom" are the ones who become humble like children (18:1–5). How significant this truth is for Matthew is evident in Jesus' extensive discussions with the Jewish leaders in Jerusalem during Holy Week. There he issues a scathing rebuke to those Pharisees and scribes who take pride in their positions of leadership and power. Then Jesus offers a solemn warning to all who wish to be his disciples: "All who exalt themselves will be humbled, and all who humble themselves will be exalted" (23:12).

The Life of Faith: Some Characteristics of a Disciple's Life

The Sermon on the Mount in chapters 5–7 of Matthew provide the most comprehensive description of what doing God's will means in practice. Not surprisingly, given the significance of humility just mentioned, this virtue is praised explicitly in the third beatitude: "Blessed are the meek." At the same time, it can be argued that humility underlies each of the other beatitudes as well (5:3–12). Take, for example, the fifth beatitude, "Blessed are the merciful, for they will receive mercy." It is those who are humble who can be merciful, and Matthew stresses *mercy* forcefully in Jesus' preaching. For instance, when the Jewish leaders question him about sharing a meal with "tax collectors and sinners"—that is, those whom the Jewish leaders tended to look down on from a religious standpoint—Jesus answers, "Go and learn what this means, 'I desire mercy, not sacrifice'" (9:10–13).

This quotation comes from the prophet Hosea (6:6) and echoes a theme that appears regularly in the Hebrew Scriptures. The point is that religious practices are meaningless unless they are accompanied by characteristics like mercy, justice, compassion, and faithfulness—qualities that involve both treating others well and honoring God. How important mercy is for Matthew is obvious from the fact that he also narrates a second story in which Jesus, questioned again by the Jewish leaders, repeats this same quotation from Hosea (12:7).

Along with mercy, there is another virtue that Matthew wishes to feature in Jesus' teaching about discipleship. That is, of course, *love*. Matthew, along with Mark and Luke, records the familiar story of the man who poses a question to Jesus about the greatest commandment in the Scriptures. Jesus replies, "You shall love the Lord your God with all your heart, and with all your soul, and with all your mind." Then he adds a second command, "You shall love your neighbor as yourself" (22:37–40).

Jesus draws these two commands from Deuteronomy 6:5 and Leviticus 19:18 respectively, and they serve as a perfect summary of the thrust of biblical teaching. In fact, these commands fit exactly the pattern of the Ten Commandments. As has often been noted, the first four commandments speak of our relation to the Lord God, and the last six refer to how we interact with other human beings (Exodus 20:1–17). The structure of the Ten Commandments, consequently, is built on love for God and love for other human beings.

However, beyond recording this story, which Matthew shares with Mark and Luke, it is clear that Matthew wishes to place still greater emphasis on love. We see his special interest as he narrates the story of the rich young man (19:16–22). Once again, both Mark and Luke also contain the account. When the rich man asks Jesus to specify the commandments he needs to keep in order to "have eternal life," all three Gospels indicate that Jesus gives examples from the Ten Commandments. Matthew, however, inserts one additional phrase that is not found in the other Gospels, "Also, you shall love your neighbor as yourself" (19:19). Disciples, above all, are those who love one another.

The Church: How Then Shall We Live Today?
Humility, mercy, and love serve as the focal points for a life of discipleship. However, they often seem to be in short supply in the contemporary world, and often enough in our churches. Love, in particular, is especially hard because of an additional pronouncement of Jesus that Matthew includes in the Sermon on the Mount, "You have heard that it was said, 'You shall love your neighbor and hate your enemy.' But I say to you, Love your enemies and pray

for those who persecute you" (5:44). The Father in heaven, Jesus continues, does good to the evil and the righteous alike, and God's children, those who follow Jesus, must do likewise (5:45-48).

Sadly, Jesus' command to "love your enemies" appears to go unheeded much of the time in our churches. Instead, we often hear about disputes, anger, and irreconcilable breaks within congregations, or competition and splits between denominations, or distaste bordering on hatred for other racial groups, political parties, or entire nations.

Matthew appears to anticipate this problem in followers of Jesus. While he presents the twelve as models of discipleship, he often portrays them as failing to follow Jesus adequately. They are fearful when a storm strikes the Sea of Galilee while Jesus continues to sleep in the boat (8:23-27); they express concern about who will be greatest in the heavenly kingdom (18:1); they resist a woman who wishes to anoint Jesus' feet (26:6-13); and they act in ways that lead Jesus more than once to label them, "You of little faith" (for example, 16:8).

In Matthew, Simon Peter becomes the prime example of the successes and failures of those who wish to be disciples of Jesus. He emerges as the acknowledged leader of the twelve disciples, and Matthew often mentions him speaking to Jesus on behalf of the others. Peter can express great faith, for instance when he attempts to walk on water with Jesus (14:28-33) or when he responds to Jesus' question about his identity with the declaration, "You are the Messiah, the Son of the living God" (16:16). But unfortunately, on the water Peter loses his courage and begins to sink below the surface, and he follows up his "great confession" by rebuking Jesus for saying that he is going to Jerusalem to suffer, die, and rise from the dead. Famously, when Jesus is arrested, Peter "follows at a distance" but then denies Jesus three times (26:58-75).

Peter's failing faith here is a poignant example of how difficult it can be for disciples to put into practice Jesus' cautionary words earlier in Matthew, "Whoever does not take up the cross and follow me is not worthy of me" (10:38). The risks for those who want to follow Jesus are evident in these words. As we know, not just the earliest disciples, but many in every century and in many lands since then, have faced persecution and death because of their faith. In Western countries, we have mostly been spared such threats, but it would be wise for us to ask ourselves what threats, dangers, or risks might face us as individuals and as the church in a society that has become progressively more polarized, cynical, and superficial.

For Reflection and Action

1. Look back through this chapter at the statements Jesus makes to the disciples. Choose one or two that seem most striking to you. Imagine yourself as one of the disciples hearing these words for the first time. What might your thoughts and feelings be about his words? Now reflect on those words and their meaning for your own life. *Place following Jesus above any other commitment. Whoever loves mother, father, son or daughter more than Jesus, not worthy of Jesus.*

2. How do you react to Jesus' language about putting our relationship with him before father, mother, and family, and how can you put this into practice in your day-to-day life? *Hard to accept. Thru prayer, bible study and worship service*

3. One of Matthew's intentions in writing this Gospel was to present the disciples as models for later followers of Jesus. Think of some ways that they might serve as models—both positively and negatively—for you. *Show more humility, mercy, justice, compassion, faithfulness and love of God and love for other human beings*

4. In many places around the globe today, following Jesus—taking up his cross—may lead to persecution and death. What dangers and risks might discipleship bring us in our circumstances? *Risking our lives as we practice righteousness, humility and love even for our enemies, Hatred for other racial groups and distrust among political parties.*

Matthew considered the Scriptures he knew as tied inseparably to Jesus and his identity (as traditional theology, speaking of the Old and New Testaments, has always maintained).

Chapter 5

Living Close to the Scriptures

Scripture

Matthew 7:13–29   contains the last section of the Sermon on the Mount, which focuses on the kind of life that is required for entrance to the kingdom.

Matthew 12:15–21   gives one example of the many times that Matthew quotes from the Hebrew Scriptures to show how Jesus as Messiah is the fulfilment of those Scriptures.

Matthew 17:1–8   relates the "Transfiguration," where Jesus meets with Moses and Elijah, who are understood as the human representatives of the Law and the Prophets in the Hebrew Scriptures.

Matthew 22:34–46   presents one of the encounters when the Jewish leaders seek to test Jesus but discover that his insight and knowledge of the Scriptures surpasses theirs.

Matthew 23:1–28   records some of Jesus' most scathing rebukes of the Pharisees and scribes for their misinterpretations of the Law.

Prayer

Dear God, as the psalmist wrote centuries ago, "Your word is a lamp to my feet and a light to my path" (119:105). I thank you that you have not wished for us to walk in darkness as we seek to be Jesus' disciples. Rather by your grace you have given Jesus as the Light of the World, and by his Word in the Scriptures, he has provided light to guide us along our paths. By your Spirit, illumine my mind to understand the words I read, and the guidance I need, to be a faithful follower of your Son. In Jesus' name. Amen.

Introduction

When Jesus replies to the question about the greatest commandment in the Scriptures, he quotes the commandments to love God and to love our neighbor, and comments, "On these two commandments hang all the law and the prophets" (22:40). The phrase "the law and the prophets" served as a cover term for the Hebrew Scriptures. Note that the word "Law"—which refers to the first five books in the Hebrew Scriptures, Genesis through Deuteronomy—translates the word "Torah" in Hebrew. This word would be better translated as "instruction" or "teaching," because it encompasses not just law but also stories, poetry, and the like. Note that "Law" could also be used to refer to the entirety of the Hebrew Scriptures. By the time of Jesus, those Scriptures comprised nearly all the books that Christians now know as the Old Testament.

Just like Christians today, Jewish groups sometimes disagreed vigorously about whether various beliefs were taught in their Scriptures. A good example is belief in a general resurrection and the afterlife. Neither of these appears clearly in the Hebrew Scriptures, but in the two centuries prior to Jesus' birth, various Jewish groups adopted both. For example, the Pharisees supported these teachings. Their opponents, the Sadducees, took a more conservative position: since neither belief could be found in the Torah, both should be rejected.

Famously, the Pharisees also focused attention on proper interpretation of the Torah, striving to apply its specific laws as precisely as possible. These applications became known as "traditions of the fathers." In the aftermath of the fall of Jerusalem to the Romans in 70 A.D., the Pharisees' approach to the law, carried on by the rabbis, came to define Judaism as we still know it today. Kosher food laws and Sabbath observance are well-known examples.

The common people followed Torah, too, but usually more loosely, and so they were often looked down on by the Pharisees. Because Jesus and his followers came from the common folk, the Pharisees skeptically scrutinized his preaching and actions. To be fair to them, their original intent was praiseworthy. They wished wholeheartedly to follow God's instruction as completely as possible.

A Basic Theme: Matthew's Approach to Scripture

If the author of Matthew is anything at all, he is a student of the Hebrew Scriptures. It is easy to overlook just how fully the entire Gospel is imbued with the religious language and thought-world of those writings. Matthew regularly quotes passages verbatim, often naming the book explicitly, but sometimes he simply assumes that his readers will recognize the source of the quotation. A good example appears in Matthew's account of the dispute between Jesus and the Pharisees, when he admonishes them to, "go and learn what this means, 'I desire mercy, not sacrifice'" (9:13). Matthew includes this quote a second time (12:7), but in neither instance does he feel a need to name the source—the prophet Hosea (Hosea 6:6).

Along with quoting Scripture directly, Matthew also often alludes to scriptural texts, as in the words of Jesus that "many will come from east and west" to be part of the kingdom of heaven (8:11). This phrase comes closest to the wording of Psalm 107:3, but slight variations can be found in other places in the Hebrew Scriptures.

Also significant is Matthew's tendency to emphasize that important events in Jesus' life either have been foretold in or fulfil a specific passage of the Scriptures. You can see this readily in the early chapters of Matthew, for example in the prophecy that the Messiah will be born in Bethlehem (2:6) or the identification of John the Baptist with Isaiah's proclamation of a "a voice crying in the wilderness" (3:1–3). A particularly lovely example occurs when Matthew relates that Jesus, seeking to avoid conflict with the religious leaders, heals many in the crowds that followed him, telling them not to talk about his ministry (12:15–21). Matthew interprets Jesus' action here as fulfilling a passage in Isaiah known as the "first servant song," where the prophet speaks of God's servant as one who is gentle and kind, who does not "wrangle or cry aloud" (compare Isaiah 42:1–4).

Still more fundamental for Matthew is the inner connection he makes between Jesus himself and the Hebrew Scriptures. At the

Transfiguration, Jesus speaks with Moses and Elijah (17:1–8). For Israel, the two represent, respectively, the Law and the prophets. When the voice from heaven calls Jesus the "beloved Son" and commands the disciples to "listen to him," Jesus is identified definitively as the authoritative interpreter of the Scriptures. The Sermon on the Mount affirms this, too, when Jesus introduces specific commandments with the words, "You have heard that it was said." Then he proclaims, "But *I* say to you" (5:21–48). The entire Sermon amounts to Jesus' authoritative exposition of the meaning and application of the Hebrew Scriptures.

For Matthew, then, Jesus is the authoritative interpreter of the Scriptures. He affirms this, too, in the conclusion to the Sermon on the Mount: "The crowds were astounded at his teaching, for he taught them as one having authority, and not as their scribes" (7:28–29). Ultimately for Matthew, that authority is founded on the reality that Jesus is the Messiah, the Son of God. It is Jesus' identity that justifies his final words to the disciples in this Gospel: "All authority in heaven and on earth has been given to me" (28:18).

The Life of Faith: Our Approach to Scripture

Matthew's love for Scripture and his profound knowledge of it are unmistakable. He wrote at a time, of course, before official Christian Scriptures had come into existence. Thus, Matthew looks to the Hebrew Scriptures for insight into both Jesus' identity and the actions that accord with living as a disciple. As the writings of the New Testament gradually came into existence, believers in Jesus gained a much more specific picture of Jesus and the meaning of Christian life. We cannot know whether Matthew realized that he was composing a book that would itself become "Scripture," but his work quickly became one of the central writings in the New Testament. It has always played a major role in proclaiming Jesus as the Messiah, the One who was foretold in the "first testament."

For Christians today, Matthew's orientation to the Scriptures is instructive. Like him, as we come to know the Scriptures, we will learn to recognize what Jesus' admonition to "do the will of the Father" means in practical terms. Nevertheless, we must qualify this statement in two directions. First, scriptural guidance for our lives does not mean that we will know precisely what to do in every situation. This is the danger that Matthew highlights in Jesus' disputes with the Pharisees. Their attempts to apply the commandments of Torah in ever-increasing detail sometimes led to "laying heavy burdens" on people, focusing on minor items rather than on "weightier matters of the Law," and forgetting that matters of the heart are more significant than external appearances (23:4–28). Such exactitude about keeping commandments can lead to what has traditionally been called "legalism." The outcome of this approach is usually that the law becomes so significant that human beings suffer.

Second, focusing on the heart and love does not, as Matthew demonstrates, allow for a lax approach to following the commandments. Recall the warning in the Sermon on the Mount about the necessity of practicing a "greater righteousness" than that of the scribes and Pharisees (5:20). Likewise, doing marvelous works will be of no help to those who do not do "the will of my Father who is in heaven" (7:21–23). Our task, therefore, is to avoid both extremes: legalism and laxity. The starting point for putting this into practice is to follow Jesus' two principles recorded by Matthew, the so-called "Golden Rule"—"In everything do to others as you would have them do to you" (7:12)—along with the twofold commandment to love God and love our neighbor (22:37–40).

Beyond this, Matthew's own example suggests that disciples today should immerse ourselves in the Scriptures. This will mean acquiring an overview of the whole arc of the biblical story, gaining some acquaintance with its main people and events, and seeking to apply the stories and teachings to our own situations. The long-term study of the Scriptures that this requires can occur in various settings, sometimes privately and sometimes with a group. However we structure our meditation on Scripture, almost certainly such continuing study will foster in us the same love for the Bible that we witness in Matthew.

The Church: The Scriptures in the Church Today

If, as most scholars believe, the Christian community in which Matthew resided was situated in a Hellenistic-Jewish environment, Matthew would certainly have been well acquainted with Greco-Roman culture. Nevertheless, in his portrait of the Messiah Jesus, Matthew draws only from the Jewish Scriptures. They constitute the authority for each of the themes he wishes to highlight in his Gospel. By saying this, I do not intend to devalue either Hellenistic or present-day fields of study. I mean only to indicate that the church today needs to maintain the primacy of scriptural authority for what the Reformed theological tradition has often called our understanding of "faith and life."

Stated differently, the physical and life sciences can contribute much to our understanding of the world around us and our own nature as human beings—not the least regarding how we think, feel, and act as religious beings. Yet if the Scriptures are to serve for us as they did for Matthew and the church in his day, they need to occupy the central place in our congregational life. Other valuable sources of knowledge, including the multitude of self-help books and Internet articles in our culture, must not replace the Scriptures as the primary source material for interpreting Jesus and his message.

This entails several things for our congregations. Perhaps we will need to put renewed emphasis on some traditional practices, such as reading extensive selections from the Scriptures in worship services, assuring that the major focus of weekly sermons is the interpretation of biblical passages, and enabling people to overcome "biblical illiteracy" by helping them learn and understand the biblical narrative.

Matthew's own use of the Hebrew Scriptures should remind us that this "older testament" is not superseded by the New Testament. Christians, unfortunately, have sometimes assumed that it is no longer central to Christian faith. A subtle example may be the tendency in some congregations to omit an "Old Testament reading" from the liturgy, either altogether or occasionally. Matthew's continual reference to the Hebrew Scriptures, however, is a reminder that we can only appreciate the person and ministry of Jesus fully if we also keep an eye on the Hebrew Scriptures.

Matthew's use of Scripture can be an example for the church today in another regard. When we face disagreement on a significant concern, especially one that involves our public witness on divisive issues, the church must not simply recite texts in a literalistic way but rather seek to understand principles in the Scriptures that bear on the issue. In so doing, we will be following

Jesus' own example in Matthew. He places Sabbath observance within the context of peoples' needs (12:1 and following), offers the "Golden Rule" as guidance for our actions (7:12), and holds up the commandments to love God and neighbor as the core of the Torah (22:34–40). Naturally, when we seek to apply principles to contemporary issues, we will often arrive at different, possibly contradictory, conclusions. Yet during such disagreements on interpretation, Matthew reminds us that disciples should continue to follow another of Jesus' admonitions: "Love one another, even your enemies!"

For Reflection and Action

1. Read Matthew 7:13–27 two or three times. What words, phrases, or ideas jump out at you? Choose one of these to concentrate on, and ask yourself what it means. How is it relevant to your own life? What might the Spirit be asking you to do specifically?

Not everyone will enter the kingdom of heaven, but only the one who does the will of my Father in heaven. Love God & your neighbor. Follow Golden Rule. Do to others as you would have them do to you

2. In the disputes between Jesus and the Pharisees about proper observance of the Sabbath, Jesus supports his actions with an appeal to the Scriptures, while at the same time declaring that "the Son of Man is lord of the sabbath" (12:8). How do you think this statement relates to his identity as Messiah and his relation to the Scriptures?

It is lawful to do good on Sabbath. I desire mercy, not sacrifice, Jesus said. He continued to heal people on the Sabbath

3. These days, many bemoan the "biblical illiteracy" in our congregations. Would you want to place yourself in that category? What are the main challenges you, or others you know, face in living close to the Scriptures, and what might help you overcome those challenges?

do not want to, but I am biblical illiterate. Need to study bible more. Continue w/ bible study. Continue church services.

4. If you think about your congregation, in what ways do you see an intentional emphasis on founding its life and activities on the Bible? Where might it be wise to put increased emphasis on the Scriptures, and what leads you to that conclusion?

Spend more time reading Old Testament — gives a firm foundation for New Testament. Stress actions in #1 above

given insight into Jesus identity & actions needed to living as a disciple

Much of Matthew's Gospel focuses on the need to accept Gentiles. At the same time, Jews remain part of the church too. Both belong to the church on an equal footing.

Chapter 6

Welcoming All

Scripture

Matthew 15:1–28 indicates that what matters in morality for Jesus is especially a person's internal attitude, and it relates the faith a foreign woman shows in seeking Jesus' help.

Matthew 18:1–14 stresses the need for disciples to be humble like children and to treat "little ones" well, following the model of the shepherd who seeks out the one sheep that is lost.

Matthew 20:1–28 relates a parable about God's grace to all, along with teaching about Jesus' coming suffering and the need for disciples to be like him.

Matthew 21:28–22:14 records more parables focusing on who will be accepted into the kingdom and hinting at the awful results of the coming rejection of Jesus.

Matthew 27:1–28:20 narrates the final events of Jesus' trials, his execution, the resurrection, and the "Great Commission" to his disciples.

Prayer

God of peace, out of your great love you have made all people in your image. You have proclaimed your desire that all may live together as brothers and sisters in your family, the church. Yet we

41

are aware that, living in a broken world, we often overlook others, and too often look down on them. Forgive me, my God, when I have spoken critically of other groups or have been less than accepting of those whom I meet. Help me to follow Jesus' example in his love and service for all people he encountered. In his name, I pray. Amen.

Introduction

Two stories in the Hebrew Scriptures are foundational for Israel's early origins. In Genesis, God calls Abraham to go to a "land that I will show you," where God will give him many descendants and make him a blessing to all nations (12:1–3). Then, in the book of Exodus, Moses leads Abraham's descendants, now a sizable people, out of slavery in Egypt to settle in the "promised land." Together, these two accounts underlie Israel's consciousness as a "chosen people," destined by God for a special role in the world. In Israel's early years, this claim did not result in clear-cut separation from other peoples. For instance, although the Moabites to the east were excoriated as enemies of the Lord (Deuteronomy 23:3), we also read about a Moabite woman, Ruth, who settles in Bethlehem and ends up as an ancestor of King David (Ruth 4:21–22).

Through the centuries, however, the sense of differentiation among peoples increased. Especially in the aftermath of the destruction of Jerusalem and the exile to Babylon in 586 B.C., the people who resettled Jerusalem some fifty years later felt not only vulnerable to attack but also culturally and religiously different from other nations. To protect Jewish identity from being swallowed up by the masses of foreign peoples who surrounded them, Ezra, who governed Jerusalem, later tightened up the requirements to follow the commandments of Torah. More ominously, he also required that Jewish males marry only within the community. This resulted in a tragic demand that Jews who had already married non-Jewish women must divorce them, sending both the women and their children away (Ezra 10).

This distaste for marriages with outsiders was also clear regarding the people who lived in the old Northern Kingdom. When the Assyrian Empire destroyed the capital city, Samaria, in 722 B.C., they deported many of the inhabitants and resettled people from other nations in the land. Over time, mixed marriages occurred among these peoples. Although the inhabitants continued to worship the Lord God, Jews to the south in Judah considered them tainted. Animosity toward "Samaritans" continued unabated over the following centuries. Thus, in the time of Jesus, Jews continued to avoid contact with both Samaritans and Gentiles whenever possible.

A Basic Theme: Jesus' Acceptance of Undervalued People

On the surface, it might appear that Jesus himself holds these same attitudes toward non-Jews. When he sends the disciples on something of a "training mission" to preach and heal, he instructs them not to go among Gentiles and Samaritans (10:5–6). Later, near the Gentile cities of Tyre and Sidon, a Canaanite woman begs Jesus to heal her daughter. He seems to speak severely to her: "It is not fair to take the children's food and throw it to the dogs" (15:26). However, her wry response leads Jesus to praise her "great faith" and heal her daughter.

Retelling this story from Mark, Matthew adds a sentence to the dialogue which may hold the key to his understanding of Jesus' intentions: "I was sent only to the lost sheep of the house of Israel" (15:24). In a similar vein to the apostle Paul, who wrote, "the Jew first and also the Greek" (Romans 2:10), Matthew appears to picture two stages in the proclamation of the gospel. Matthew portrays Jesus' own earthly ministry as focusing on the Jews. Then, in the context of his resurrection and ascension, Jesus commissions the disciples—now apostles—to "Go and make disciples of *all nations*" (28:19).

In fact, Matthew's Gospel includes numerous hints that Gentiles will be welcome in the kingdom. Early on, Matthew relates the story of wise men coming to worship the baby Jesus (2:1–2). Later stories mention a centurion whose servant needs healing (8:5–13); another centurion who expresses his faith at the cross (27:54); and Pilate's wife, whose dream convinces her that Jesus is innocent (27:19).

Not only does Matthew stress that foreigners, including both Gentiles and Samaritans, are welcome in the kingdom of heaven, but at various points in the Gospel, he also underscores the significance of other groups who were regularly undervalued. Like most peoples, Israel's patriarchal culture tied the worth of women to male members of their household. While Matthew does not seek to change the cultural pattern, he does narrate various interactions that show Jesus' esteem for women. Note his compassion for the woman who sought healing for a long-term flow of blood (9:20–22); his approval of the woman who wishes to anoint his feet with oil (26:6–13); and the praise for the Canaanite woman just mentioned (15:21–28).

Jesus commends each of these women for their strong faith. This approval appears all the greater in light of the regular accusations that he directs against the Jewish leaders for their lack of faith. In addition, observe Matthew's comment that many women were present when Jesus was crucified. The remark that they had followed him from Galilee shows clearly that Jesus welcomed women and the role they could play in his ministry (27:55).

Matthew refers to other groups, too, who were considered of less value in society but receive approval from Jesus. Children (18:1–6), those in need (10:42), and "tax collectors and sinners" (9:10–13) are all considered worthy of Jesus' time and attention. His closing words in the parable of the Lost Sheep apply to all: "It is not the will of your Father in heaven that one of these little ones should be lost" (18:14). Whatever the social, racial, or religious status of the group, the message of Jesus in Matthew is evident: all deserve compassion and affirmation, and all are welcome in the kingdom of heaven.

The Life of Faith: Living as God's Family

Earlier, we noted that, as Jesus describes participation in the kingdom of heaven, he comments, "Many will come from east and west" (8:11). This expression can be found in slightly different wording in several places in the Hebrew Scriptures. It is similar to other phrases, such as "from the rising of the sun to its setting" (Psalm 113:3; Malachi 1:11) or "to the ends of the earth" (Psalm 48:10). In context, these expressions usually indicate that the whole world owes God praise as the glorious creator of all things. Implicitly, they also suggest both that Israel is only a small people within the whole world, and that God's mercy also extends to all other peoples, that is, the Gentiles, in that larger world.

At various places in the Hebrew Scriptures and especially in the Prophets there are specific references to God's concern for the

Gentiles. The prophet Micah, for example, proclaims that many nations will exclaim, "Come, let us go up to the mountain of the LORD, to the house of the God of Jacob" (4:2). However, such passages are set amid many others that announce God's judgment on Gentiles for their evil treatment of Israel. It is these latter passages that undergirded the habitual distaste for Gentiles that we spoke of earlier.

It is no wonder, then, that Jesus' proclamation that Gentiles, too, are welcome in the kingdom was difficult even for his own disciples to accept. By the time Matthew was writing, the church already included large numbers of Gentiles. Given the traditional distaste of Jews toward Gentiles, it is not surprising that there was often friction within the Christian communities. Thus Matthew, in composing this Gospel as a "manual of discipleship," stresses the need for members of the churches to hold to their obligations both to serve and to love one another.

Living as disciples in our own communities, we are not immune to friction and animosity any more than were the original disciples. However, Jesus' attitude of welcoming Gentiles, upholding women, and valuing all people remains incumbent on us. Differences in personalities, political views, social status, racial-ethnic backgrounds, and the like can easily lead to preference for some and avoidance of others. Nevertheless, Jesus' words about his own "family" are applicable here: "Whoever does the will of my Father in heaven is my brother and sister and mother" (12:50). In that others are also striving to be followers of Jesus, they are also part of our "family" too.

There are two things to note specifically in this context. First, the term "followers of Jesus," or his "family," embraces not just those in our own denomination of local congregation but all those in nearby congregations, in other denominations, and in other nations. This statement is perhaps obvious, but in practice it has proven easy to forget due to our human tendencies to provincialism and insularity.

Second, this family connection implies not simply that we accept others who are different but that we respect even "the least of these" (25:45) as equally valuable in God's eyes. We will also need to guard against acting like Jesus' disciples, who were competing to be "greatest" in the kingdom. In other words, respecting others within our communities also requires not feeling superior to them or simply tolerating their presence among us. This brings us back to Jesus' remark that the greatest in the kingdom of heaven is in fact the one who practices humility (18:1–4).

The Church: The Basis for Welcoming All

It has become popular, particularly in the scholarly world, to speak of the anti-Judaism or anti-Semitism of some New Testament writings, including Matthew. On the surface, there appears to be justification for this accusation. This Gospel often speaks in harsh terms against the Jewish leaders, especially when Jesus chastises them as "you snakes, you brood of vipers," who are just like their ancestors, "who murdered the prophets" (23:31–33).

For Matthew, the implication is that the Jewish leaders will also kill Jesus. The same suggestion underlies the parable of the Wicked Tenants who eventually kill the owner's son (21:33–44). Both Mark and Luke contain this parable, but Matthew includes a further comment by Jesus: "Therefore I tell you, the kingdom of God will be taken away from you and given to a people that produces the fruits of the kingdom" (21:43). This and other passages in Matthew imply a rejection of Israel as God's chosen people and their replacement by the church, that is, the followers of Jesus, made up mostly of Gentiles.

The rupture becomes final at Jesus' trial when the people in the crowd cry out, "His blood be on us and on our children!" (27:25). It is tragic that this oath has been misused by many followers of Jesus through the centuries to persecute and discriminate against Jewish people. However, nothing in Matthew justifies any such actions. As we have seen, Matthew was probably Jewish himself, and his community was likely made up of both Jews and Gentiles. Matthew's viewpoint is best summarized in Jesus' words about his family consisting of all those who do "the will of my Father" (12:50). Because of continuing anti-Jewish bias in our day, our churches need to affirm in the strongest possible way that Jews as well as Gentiles are to be welcomed and valued equally in the Church of Jesus Christ.

Here we can circle back to the opening chapters of this study, where we saw that embracing Jesus and seeking the kingdom meant something radically different from the normal expectations of the time. As Jesus explained to the disciples on the road to Jerusalem, "The Son of Man came not to be served but to serve, and to give his life a ransom for many" (20:28). That remark points forward to the final events that Matthew narrates in this Gospel: Jesus' trials, crucifixion, and resurrection (chapters 26–28). At the trials, the high priest questions whether Jesus is the "Son of God" (26:63). Later Pilate asks sarcastically if he is "the King of the Jews" (27:11). These days, living in a cultural milieu that often portrays truth as relative, our churches must answer those twin questions with a resounding "Yes."

Matthew, then, emphasizes that Jesus is indeed the Son of God and king. Yet Matthew's final chapters show how differently Jesus conducts himself as one with absolute authority. For in the horror of the trials and the crucifixion, along with the later joy of the resurrection and ascension, Jesus displays vividly what he taught in his ministry. And it is these astounding events that open the door so that the original chosen people, along with all other people, too, are welcome to become his disciples.

For Reflection and Action

1. Reflect on the themes we have discussed in the six chapters of this study. Which theme speaks most strongly to you? More generally, what thoughts or ideas stand out? Spend some time thinking about one or two of these. How do they help you—in the lovely words attributed to Richard of Chichester in the thirteenth century— "to see Thee [Christ] more clearly, love Thee more dearly, and follow Thee more nearly, day by day"?

2. It is ironic that, while Christians have sent missionaries to faraway lands to proclaim Jesus as Messiah, we have often been unwelcoming to those folks when they move into our own neighborhoods. Why is this, do you think?

3. Matthew stresses the role of women in Jesus' life and ministry. Notice that the genealogy of Jesus in chapter 1 names several women. This is highly unusual in genealogies. Why do you think Matthew names these women? You may want to consult a Bible dictionary to reflect on what is especially significant about each of them.

Judah's daughter-in-law

Tamar - mother of Perez + Zerah
Rahab mother of Boaz
× Ruth " " Obed

Mary - mother of Jesus

4. Are you aware of any friction or animosity in your own congregation? What about members of other congregations? Or what about other groups of people? How might you work to eliminate conflict and replace it with welcome and support for one another?

racial conflicts
income differences
political differences

Follow Jesus' example in his love and service for all people

Ruth - a Moabite widow who went w/her mother-in-law Naomi to Bethlehem. Gathered gleanings from the field of Boaz, whom she later married.

Group Gatherings

Eva Stimson

Embracing Jesus
as Messiah

Main Idea

Matthew presents Jesus as the long-hoped for Messiah, but one who will do much more than reign over Israel and the world. Jesus also brings redemption from human weaknesses and failures, as he sacrifices himself by dying on behalf of humanity and thus offering forgiveness of sins. We can trust him to be with us always.

Preparing to Lead

- Read and reflect on chapter 1, "Embracing Jesus as Messiah."
- Review this plan for the group gathering, and select the questions and activities that you will use.
- What other questions, issues, or themes occur to you from your reflection?

Gathering

- Provide name tags and pens as people arrive.
- Provide simple refreshments; ask a volunteer to bring refreshments for the next gathering.
- Agree on simple ground rules and organization (for example, time to begin and end; location for gatherings; welcoming all points of view; confidentiality; and so on). Encourage participants to bring their study books and Bibles.
- Review the gathering format: Gathering, Opening Worship, Conversation, and Conclusion.

Opening Worship

Prayer (unison)

Gracious God, who created the world and all in it, we praise your name for your marvelous works, for stars and planets, for seas and mountains, for us and all living creatures. That you created us in your very image is wonderful beyond words. In the face of our faults and failures, that you have sent your Son to redeem us is far more than we could ever imagine, much less deserve. At the beginning of this study, we ask that you grant us insight to understand Jesus' teachings more fully. Draw us closer to him, the Messiah, your own beloved Son. Amen.

Prayerful, Reflective Reading
- Read Matthew 11:25–30 aloud.
- Invite all to reflect for a few minutes in silence.
- After reflection time, invite all to listen for a word or phrase as the passage is read again and to reflect on that word or phrase in silence.
- Read the passage a third time, asking all to offer a silent prayer following the reading.
- Invite volunteers to share the word or phrase that spoke most deeply to them. *all things have been committed to me by my Father. gentle and humble*

Prayer
Loving God, hear our prayers today as we seek to follow you more faithfully:

(*spoken prayers may be offered*)

Hear us now as we pray together, saying, Our Father . . .

Conversation
- Introduce chapter 1, "Embracing Jesus as Messiah." Share observations, reflections, and insights.
- Review the Introduction (pp. 2–3), noting questions about the sources and authorship of Matthew. On a sheet of newsprint write "Messiah." Add to the sheet other terms associated with Messiah ("Christ," "anointed one," "Son of David," "Jesus"). Ask:

  How did Jesus differ from the type of Messiah Israel expected?

- Review "A Basic Theme: What Sort of Messiah Is Jesus?" (pp. 3–4). Form three groups. Assign each group one of the following passages: Matthew 8:1–27; Matthew 11:25—12:14; and

Matthew 20:20–28. Have each group make a list of things the passage reveals about Jesus as Messiah. Share the lists. Add other names or descriptions of Jesus to the newsprint list started earlier ("healer," "feeder," "miracle worker," "servant," "Son of God," "Emmanuel").

- Review "The Life of Faith: Trust in the Lord of Life" (pp. 4–5). Key points:
    a. Matthew repeatedly emphasizes that Jesus, as the Son of God, deserves the same honor as does God.
    b. Jesus claims the same power as God to forgive sins, and his death brings about the possibility of forgiveness.
    c. Trusting in Jesus offers comfort and security in an uncertain world; Jesus, the Messiah, is with us always.
- Review "The Church: Confessing the Messiah in Current Culture" (pp. 5–7). Ask:

  How does Jesus challenge human claims to ultimate authority—in the Gospel of Matthew and in our world today? How do people today tend to view authority? God's messiah is the true king

  How can the church proclaim the authority of God and God's Son, Jesus the Messiah, without appearing to be autocratic itself? Must real 3e that ultimate authority is in God alone and in Jesus.

- Have participants pair up and discuss the fourth question in For Reflection and Action (p. 7), also considering other titles for Jesus that you have listed during this group gathering.

Conclusion
Invite participants to pray and reflect silently on the "Jesus Prayer," as suggested in For Reflection and Action (p. 7).

Passing the Peace
The peace of Christ be with you.
   And also with you.

Seeking the Kingdom of Heaven

Main Idea
While the final fullness of the kingdom of heaven will be unveiled in the future, the seeds of the kingdom are already present and active in the world. Matthew calls us to look for signs of the kingdom today and to be ready for Jesus' return, recognizing that all the world's institutions, including the church, are subject to God alone.

Preparing to Lead
- Read and reflect on chapter 2, "Seeking the Kingdom of Heaven."
- Review this plan for the group gathering, and select the questions and activities that you will use.
- If you plan to use the "Pick a Parable" activity to study the parables in Matthew 13, write the name and Scripture reference for each parable on an index card or strip of paper. Place these in a box or bag labeled "Pick a Parable."
- What other questions, issues, or themes occur to you from your reflection?

Gathering
- Provide name tags and pens as people arrive.
- Provide simple refreshments; ask a volunteer to bring refreshments for the next gathering.
- Agree on simple ground rules and organization (for example, time to begin and end; location for gatherings; welcoming all points of view; confidentiality; and so on). Encourage participants to bring their study books and Bibles.

- Review the gathering format: Gathering, Opening Worship, Conversation, and Conclusion.

Opening Worship
Prayer (unison)
God Most High, we give thanks to you and praise your name as the Ruler of heaven and earth. All angels and archangels and the hosts who dwell in heaven live in peace, rejoicing in your goodness and delighting in your love and mercies. Here on earth, however, nation wars against nation, and people seek power over one another. Through the power of Jesus, the Messiah, we pray that you will cause your kingdom to come on this earth as it is in heaven. Let humility reign, and grant that all of us may serve one another. In the name of Jesus, we pray. Amen.

Prayerful, Reflective Reading
- Read Matthew 13:1–9 aloud.
- Invite all to reflect for a few minutes in silence.
- After reflection time, invite all to listen for a word or phrase as the passage is read again and to reflect on that word or phrase in silence. *whoever has ears, let them hear.*
- Read the passage a third time, asking all to offer a silent prayer following the reading.
- Invite volunteers to share the word or phrase that spoke most deeply to them. *If someone hears the Word and understands it, they can spread the word to others and serve one another.*

Prayer
Loving God, hear our prayers today as we seek to follow you more faithfully:

(*spoken prayers may be offered*)

Hear us now as we pray together, saying, Our Father . . .

Conversation
- Introduce chapter 2, "Seeking the Kingdom of Heaven." Share observations, reflections, and insights.
- Review the Introduction (pp. 10–11). Emphasize the following key points:

a. The Jews hoped for a messiah who would deliver them from bondage and restore the golden age of David and Solomon.

b. From the birth and baptism of Jesus through the rest of the Gospel, Matthew emphasizes the coming of the kingdom of heaven.

c. Matthew's use of "kingdom of heaven" rather than "kingdom of God" suggests that he was Jewish and writing for a primarily Jewish audience.

d. The Greek term "kingdom" carries a more active connotation, stressing more the king's governing than his territory.

• Review "A Basic Theme: What Sort of Kingdom Is This?" (pp. 11–12). On a sheet of newsprint, write "Kingdom of Heaven." Underneath write "Already" and "Not Yet." Ask:

What are some signs that the seeds of the kingdom are already here? (How does Jesus respond to John the Baptist's question in Matthew 11:2–6? Where have you seen signs of the kingdom in your own life or in the world around you?)

What kinds of things will occur in the future kingdom? What "apocalyptic" images about the future does Jesus use in Matthew 24 and 25?

What do you think about preaching that stresses the end times, even predicting the date of Jesus' return? Are there problems with this approach?

• Review "The Life of Faith: Desiring the Kingdom" (pp. 12–13). Divide into pairs or small groups and have each group "pick a parable" (one or more) from Matthew 13 to read and explore, looking for what each parable reveals about the kingdom of heaven. Have the groups share their findings.

• Review "The Church: Whose Kingdom Does the Church Promote?" (pp. 13–15). Ask:

How does Matthew stress the ultimate authority of the kingdom of heaven?

What does the centrality of God's kingdom reveal about the status of human kingdoms and institutions? About the church?

How can we counter the human tendency to want to be special or better than others?

Conclusion
Invite participants to pray intentionally throughout the coming week for the coming of God's kingdom, as suggested in For Reflection and Action (p. 15).

Passing the Peace
The peace of Christ be with you.
    And also with you.
Amen.

Kingdom of Heaven

Wars and Rumors of wars — Already

nations against nations   "

Kingdom against Kingdom   "

famines and earthquakes   "

handed over to be
    persecuted and put to death

Hated by all nations
    because of God

false prophets   "

Increase of wickedness   "

Gospel of the Kingdom will
be preached in entire world   "

Fleeing Evil

Main Idea

Matthew recognizes the subtle yet destructive power of evil in the human heart as well as in social structures. Calling believers to repent and to live in a manner befitting God's kingdom, Matthew emphasizes that not just words and actions matter but also the thoughts and motives of the heart.

Preparing to Lead

- Read and reflect on chapter 3, "Fleeing Evil."
- Review this plan for the group gathering, and select the questions and activities that you will use.
- Gather newspaper and magazine clippings and/or headlines printed from the Internet that show examples of "structural evil" in society.
- What other questions, issues, or themes occur to you from your reflection?

Gathering

- Provide name tags and pens as people arrive.
- Provide simple refreshments; ask a volunteer to bring refreshments for the next gathering.
- Agree on simple ground rules and organization (for example, time to begin and end; location for gatherings; welcoming all points of view; confidentiality; and so on). Encourage participants to bring their study books and Bibles.
- Review the gathering format: Gathering, Opening Worship, Conversation, and Conclusion.

Opening Worship
Prayer (unison)

Righteous and gracious God, you have called all people to live according to your will, but we have often chosen evil paths, falling victim to temptations and treating others in ways that benefit us, often at their expense. We confess that we, too, have fallen far short of your will. Guard us from evil powers. Cleanse our hearts so that what we say and do may match our thoughts and desires. By your Spirit, restrain the power of evil in the world, and enable us all, but especially those of us who bear the name of Jesus, to show his love to all. Amen.

Prayerful, Reflective Reading
- Read Matthew 7:1–5 aloud.
- Invite all to reflect for a few minutes in silence.
- After reflection time, invite all to listen for a word or phrase as the passage is read again and to reflect on that word or phrase in silence.
- Read the passage a third time, asking all to offer a silent prayer following the reading.
- Invite volunteers to share the word or phrase that spoke most deeply to them. *Do not judge, or you too will be judged*

Prayer
Loving God, hear our prayers today as we seek to follow you more faithfully:

(*spoken prayers may be offered*)

Hear us now as we pray together, saying, Our Father . . .

Conversation
- Introduce chapter 3, "Fleeing Evil." Share observations, reflections, and insights. Discuss the first question in For Reflection and Action (p. 23).
- Review the Introduction (p. 18). Emphasize the following key points:
  a. For ancient Israel, the word "evil" covered a broad range of troubles, including disasters, misfortune, and illness, as well as human moral failures.

b. The biblical authors usually speak of evil, along with everything else in the creation, as under God's ultimate control.

c. The Hebrew Scriptures contain scattered references to Satan; by the time of Jesus, it had become commonplace to visualize an evil dominion headed by Satan inciting humans into all manner of sinful actions.

d. Matthew's Gospel begins with an example of evil in Herod's order to kill all baby boys in and around Bethlehem.

- Review "A Basic Theme: Why Is Evil a Problem for Humans?" (pp. 18–20). Read Matthew 4:1–11 and recall the discussion of parables in your last group gathering. Ask:

  How does Matthew emphasize the power of evil?

  How do the parables in Matthew 13 speak to evil's continuing threat to humanity? How will God deal with evil in the end?

  What does Jesus' parable of the Sheep and the Goats (Matthew 25:31–46) say about human responsibility in the face of evil?

  action of humans, good or bad, determined whose kingdom they serve

- Review "The Life of Faith: How Do We Deal with Evil?" (pp. 20–21). Divide into three groups and assign each group one of the following: Matthew 5:1–16; Matthew 5:17–48; Matthew 7:1–12 and the second question in For Reflection and Action (p. 23). Have them look for what Jesus says about evil in relation to words, actions, thoughts, and motives. Have each group share their insights.

- Review "The Church: Responding to Evil in Human Society" (pp. 21–22). Display newspaper/magazine clippings and/or news headlines from the Internet. Look for examples of "structural evil" and list these on newsprint. Discuss the third question in For Reflection and Action (p. 23).

Conclusion

Reflect on ways you may be threatened by evil as suggested in the first question in For Reflection and Action. Discuss ways to recognize the dangers so that we can hold fast to the Messiah.

Passing the Peace

The peace of Christ be with you.
    And also with you.
Amen.

Following Jesus

Main Idea
The Gospel of Matthew provides a kind of "manual for discipleship," with the disciples as models for how we should live as followers of Jesus: risking our lives as we practice righteousness, humility, and love, even for our enemies. Peter, with his strengths and weaknesses, is the prime example; we are encouraged to emulate his successes and avoid his failures.

Preparing to Lead
- Read and reflect on chapter 4, "Following Jesus."
- Review this plan for the group gathering, and select the questions and activities that you will use.
- What other questions, issues, or themes occur to you from your reflection?

Gathering
- Provide name tags and pens as people arrive.
- Provide simple refreshments; ask a volunteer to bring refreshments for the next gathering.
- Agree on simple ground rules and organization (for example, time to begin and end; location for gatherings; welcoming all points of view; confidentiality; and so on). Encourage participants to bring their study books and Bibles.
- Review the gathering format: Gathering, Opening Worship, Conversation, and Conclusion.

Opening Worship
Prayer (unison)
God of love, who calls us all to be followers of Jesus the Messiah.

That you wish us to be like those disciples whom Jesus called to himself is a gift of your grace. We know that the way of discipleship can be hard and, for some, treacherous. Yet we know, too, that your Son will always be with us. We thank you for your call to us also to be followers of Jesus. Uphold us when we fail, as the disciples did. Grant us strength to live humbly, with mercy and love for all whom we meet. In Jesus' name, we pray. Amen.

Prayerful, Reflective Reading

- Read Matthew 19:16–30 aloud.
- Invite all to reflect for a few minutes in silence.
- After reflection time, invite all to listen for a word or phrase as the passage is read again and to reflect on that word or phrase in silence.
- Read the passage a third time, asking all to offer a silent prayer following the reading.
- Invite volunteers to share the word or phrase that spoke most deeply to them.

Prayer

Loving God, hear our prayers today as we seek to follow you more faithfully:

(spoken prayers may be offered)

Hear us now as we pray together, saying, Our Father . . .

Conversation

- Introduce chapter 4, "Following Jesus." Share observations, reflections, and insights.
- Review the Introduction (pp. 26–27). On a sheet of newsprint, write "Matthew = Manual of Discipleship" and "Jesus' disciples = models for us." Ask:

    If you were writing a table of contents for Matthew's discipleship manual, what topics would you include?

- Review "A Basic Theme: What It Means to 'Follow Jesus'" (pp. 27–28). Discuss:

How do you react to Jesus' language about putting our relationship with him before father, mother, and family, and how can you put this into practice in your day-to-day life?

- Divide into three groups and assign each group one of the following passages: Matthew 9:34–39; Matthew 16:24–28; and Matthew 19:16–30. Have them list examples of hyperbole, harsh words, and either/or language. Ask:

   What is Jesus saying about discipleship? How does Jesus use these rhetorical devices to make his point?

- Review "The Life of Faith: Some Characteristics of a Disciple's Life" (pp. 28–29). On a sheet of newsprint, write "humility" and "love." Note that these are two virtues Matthew wishes to feature in Jesus' teaching about discipleship. Read aloud together the Beatitudes (Matthew 5:1–11), listening for the theme of "humility." Compare Matthew's story of the rich young man (19:16–26) with the story told in Mark 10:17–27 and Luke 18:18–27. Ask:

   What does Matthew add to the story? Why?

   How does Jesus draw from Deuteronomy 6:5 and Leviticus 19:18 in the story to summarize biblical teaching about discipleship?

   Who does Jesus tell us to love in this story? In the Sermon on the Mount (Matthew 5:43–48)? Who are some of our neighbors/enemies today?

- Review "The Church: How Then Shall We Live Today?" (pp. 29–31). Point out that Matthew presents the disciples, particularly Peter, as models of discipleship for us to learn from and emulate. Divide into two groups. Have one group read Matthew 16:13–20 and the other group read Matthew 26:69–75. Have them list Peter's strengths and weaknesses and discuss how he is a model for discipleship. Allow time for the groups to share insights.
- Return to two groups. Discuss:

One of Matthew's intentions in writing this Gospel was to present the disciples as models for later followers of Jesus. Think of some ways that they might serve as models—both positively and negatively—for you.

In many places around the globe today, following Jesus—taking up his cross—may lead to persecution and death. What dangers and risks might discipleship bring us in our circumstances?

List dangers and risks we could face in following Jesus today. Share insights with the entire group.

Conclusion
Look back through this chapter at the statements Jesus makes to the disciples as suggested in the first question in For Reflection and Action. Choose one or two that seem most striking to you. Discuss these words and their meaning for your life.

Passing the Peace
The peace of Christ be with you.
    And also with you.
Amen.

Living Close to the Scriptures

Main Idea

Matthew looks to the Hebrew Scriptures for insight into both Jesus' identity and the actions that correspond to living as a disciple; he presents Jesus as the authoritative interpreter of the Scriptures. Christians today are called to follow Matthew's example by immersing ourselves in Scripture, making it central in our congregational lives, and avoiding the extremes of legalism and laxity.

Preparing to Lead

- Read and reflect on chapter 5, "Living Close to the Scriptures."
- Review this plan for the group gathering, and select the questions and activities that you will use.
- What other questions, issues, or themes occur to you from your reflection?

Gathering

- Provide name tags and pens as people arrive.
- Provide simple refreshments; ask a volunteer to bring refreshments for the next gathering.
- Agree on simple ground rules and organization (for example, time to begin and end; location for gatherings; welcoming all points of view; confidentiality; and so on). Encourage participants to bring their study books and Bibles.
- Review the gathering format: Gathering, Opening Worship, Conversation, and Conclusion.

Opening Worship
Prayer (unison)

Dear God, as the psalmist wrote centuries ago, "Your word is a lamp to my feet and a light to my path" (119:105). We thank you that you have not wished for us to walk in darkness as we seek to be Jesus' disciples. Rather by your grace, you have given Jesus as the Light of the World, and by his Word in the Scriptures, he has provided light to guide us along our paths. By your Spirit, illumine our minds to understand the words we read, and the guidance we need, to be faithful followers of your Son. In Jesus' name, we pray. Amen.

Prayerful, Reflective Reading
- Read Matthew 17:1–8 aloud.
- Invite all to reflect for a few minutes in silence.
- After reflection time, invite all to listen for a word or phrase as the passage is read again and to reflect on that word or phrase in silence.
- Read the passage a third time, asking all to offer a silent prayer following the reading.
- Invite volunteers to share the word or phrase that spoke most deeply to them.

Prayer
Loving God, hear our prayers today as we seek to follow you more faithfully:

(*spoken prayers may be offered*)

Hear us now as we pray together, saying, Our Father . . .

Conversation
- Introduce chapter 5, "Living Close to the Scriptures." Share observations, reflections, and insights.
- Review the Introduction (pp. 34–35). On a sheet of newsprint, list the following key terms: "Hebrew Scriptures," "Law and Prophets," "Torah," "Pharisees." Discuss the meaning of these. Emphasize the following key points:
  a. "Hebrew Scriptures" has become the preferred usage in academic circles, especially because for many people "old" in "Old Testament" carries the sense of less valuable or obsolete.

b. Matthew's use of the Scriptures in relation to Jesus reveals that he considered the Scriptures he knew as anything but obsolete.

c. Matthew's use of the Hebrew Scriptures should remind us that this "older testament" is not superseded by the New Testament.

- Review "A Basic Theme: Matthew's Approach to Scripture" (pp. 35–36). Discuss:

> *In the disputes between Jesus and the Pharisees about proper observance of the Sabbath, Jesus supports his actions with an appeal to the Scriptures, while at the same time declaring that "the Son of Man is lord of the sabbath" (12:8). How do you think this statement relates to his identity as Messiah and his relation to the Scriptures?*

- Divide into groups, and have each group see how many quotations and allusions to the Hebrew Scriptures they can find in Matthew. Suggest that they begin by looking at chapters 7 and 12. Compare the lists. Ask:

> *What do these examples reveal about Matthew's attitude toward Scripture?*

> *What do they reveal about Jesus?*

> *What does the Transfiguration story (Matthew 17:1–8) reveal about the relationship of Jesus to Scripture? What words and phrases from this story stood out for you in the reading during opening worship?*

- Review "The Life of Faith: Our Approach to Scripture" (pp. 36–37). On a sheet of newsprint, write "legalism" and "laxity." Point out that these are two extremes to avoid in using Scripture today. Divide into three groups, and assign each group one of the following passages: Matthew 7:12–27; Matthew 22:34–46; and Matthew 23:1–28. Have them look for examples of legalism and laxity in following God's commandments. Have the groups share their findings. Ask:

What guiding principles does Jesus provide for those seeking to obey God's Word?

How do these apply to us today?

- Review "The Church: The Scriptures in the Church Today" (pp. 37–39). Return to small groups and have participants discuss:

  These days, many bemoan the "biblical illiteracy" in our congregations. Would you want to place yourself in that category? What are the main challenges you, or others you know, face in living close to the Scriptures, and what might help you overcome those challenges?

  If you think about your congregation, in what ways do you see an intentional emphasis on founding its life and activities on the Bible? Where might it be wise to put increased emphasis on the Scriptures, and what leads you to that conclusion?

- List two or three ways your congregation could help members grow in their use of Scripture. Rather than criticizing current practices, suggest that they start by listing helpful things already being done (Bible studies, Scripture readings in worship, vacation Bible school, etc.) and consider how to build on those.

Conclusion
Read Matthew 7:13–27 two or three times as suggested in the first question in For Reflection and Action. Concentrate on a word, phrase, or idea that resonates with you, and ask yourself what it means. How is it relevant to your own life? What might the Spirit be asking you to do specifically?

Passing the Peace
The peace of Christ be with you.
   And also with you.
Amen.

Welcoming All

Main Idea

Matthew stresses that foreigners, including both Gentiles and Samaritans, as well as undervalued groups such as women, children, those in need, and "tax collectors and sinners" are all welcome in the kingdom of heaven. Living as God's family today means humbly welcoming all, despite our differences.

Preparing to Lead

- Read and reflect on chapter 6, "Welcoming All."
- Review this plan for the group gathering, and select the questions and activities that you will use.
- What other questions, issues, or themes occur to you from your reflection?

Gathering

- Provide name tags and pens as people arrive.
- Provide simple refreshments; ask a volunteer to bring refreshments for the next gathering.
- Agree on simple ground rules and organization (for example, time to begin and end; location for gatherings; welcoming all points of view; confidentiality; and so on). Encourage participants to bring their study books and Bibles.
- Review the gathering format: Gathering, Opening Worship, Conversation, and Conclusion.

Opening Worship

Prayer (unison)

God of peace, out of your great love you have made all people in your image. You have proclaimed your desire that all may live together as brothers and sisters in your family, the church. Yet we are aware that, living in a broken world, we often overlook others, and too often look down on them. Forgive us, God, when we have spoken critically of other groups or have been less than accepting of those we meet. Help us to follow Jesus' example in his love and service for all people he encountered. In his name, we pray. Amen.

Prayerful, Reflective Reading
- Read Matthew 18:1–14 aloud.
- Invite all to reflect for a few minutes in silence.
- After reflection time, invite all to listen for a word or phrase as the passage is read again and to reflect on that word or phrase in silence.
- Read the passage a third time, asking all to offer a silent prayer following the reading.
- Invite volunteers to share the word or phrase that spoke most deeply to them. *unless you change and become like little children, you will never enter the kingdom of heaven.*

Prayer
Loving God, hear our prayers today as we seek to follow you more faithfully:

(*spoken prayers may be offered*)

Hear us now as we pray together, saying, Our Father . . .

Conversation
- Introduce chapter 6, "Welcoming All." Share observations, reflections, and insights.
- Review the Introduction (pp. 42–43). Draw a time line on newsprint to show Israel's developing sense of separation as a "chosen people." Add the following key events:
  a. God's call of Abraham
  b. Moses leading the people out of Egypt
  c. Arrival in the "promised land"
  d. Assyrian conquest leading to mixed marriages and animosity toward "Samaritans"
  e. Babylonian exile and destruction of Jerusalem
  f. Return of exiled Jews; Ezra's tightened enforcement of Torah to protect Jewish identity

- Review "A Basic Theme: Jesus' Acceptance of Undervalued People" (pp. 43–44). Discuss:

  Matthew stresses the role of women in Jesus' life and ministry. Notice that the genealogy of Jesus in chapter 1 names several women. This is highly unusual in genealogies. Why do you think Matthew names these women? You may want to consult a Bible dictionary to reflect on what is especially significant about each of them.

- Divide into several groups, and have each group search Matthew for examples of Jesus' treatment of non-Jews and other undervalued people. Suggest that they begin by looking at chapters 15, 18, 20, and 21. Compare the lists. Ask:

  What do you think about Jesus' response to the Canaanite woman (15:21–28), especially considering his Great Commission to "make disciples of all nations" (28:19)?

  How does Jesus interact with other women in Matthew's Gospel? With other undervalued groups?

  What hints do you find early in Matthew's Gospel (2:1–2) that Gentiles will be welcome in God's kingdom?

- Review "The Life of Faith: Living as God's Family" (pp. 44–46). Note that Jesus' proclamation of welcome to Gentiles was one of the biggest sources of friction within the early Christian communities. Divide into several groups and discuss:

  It is ironic that, while Christians have sent missionaries to faraway lands to proclaim Jesus as Messiah, we have often been unwelcoming to those folks when they move into our own neighborhoods. Why is this, do you think?

  Are you aware of any friction or animosity in your own congregation? Perhaps with members of other congregations? Or what about other groups of people? How might you work to eliminate conflict and replace it with welcome and support for one another?

What kinds of differences cause friction in the church today? How would Matthew challenge us to respond?

- Review "The Church: The Basis for Welcoming All" (pp. 46–47). Review the commentary in the first three paragraphs about anti-Semitism in some New Testament writings, and invite participants to respond. Reflect on the account of Jesus' trial, death, and resurrection in the final chapters of Matthew. Ask:

  How does Jesus conduct himself during these events?

  What does Jesus' conduct reveal about his identity as Messiah?

- Review key themes discussed in the six chapters of this study, listing them on newsprint. Invite participants to spend some time reflecting prayerfully on one or two themes, as suggested in For Reflection and Action (pp. 47–48).

Conclusion
Reflect on the six themes of this study as suggested in the first question in For Reflection and Action. How do they help you—in the lovely words attributed to Richard of Chichester in the thirteenth century—"to see Thee [Christ] more clearly, love Thee more dearly, and follow Thee more nearly, day by day"?

Passing the Peace
The peace of Christ be with you.
    And also with you.
Amen.

Glossary*

apocalyptic literature. From the Greek term *apokalyptein*, "to uncover, to reveal." This type of biblical literature portrays the end of the world and of human history.

Christ. From the Greek term *christos* meaning "anointed one," translated from the Hebrew *mashiah*. This is the "coming one" anticipated in the Hebrew Scriptures to initiate God's rule of righteousness. The "Christ" is seen by Christians as being Jesus of Nazareth.

church. The community or assembly of believers who profess faith in Jesus Christ.

devil/Satan. Hebrew term for "accuser" or "adversary." The devil/Satan represents the most diabolical evil in opposition to God and God's purposes.

Emmanuel. Hebrew term for "God with us." A designation for Jesus Christ (Matthew 1:23, citing Isaiah 7:14).

evil. That which opposes the will of God. Biblically, evil is seen as covering a broad range of troubles, including disasters, misfortune, and illness.

Jesus. From the Hebrew *Yehoshua'* for "Yahweh is salvation" or "God saves." This is the name given to the son of Joseph and Mary who will "save his people from their sins" (Matthew 1:21).

legalism. A system of behavior based on obedience to prescribed laws or rules, often making the law so significant that human beings suffer.

Messiah. Hebrew term meaning "anointed one" (Greek *christos*). This is the "coming one" anticipated in the Hebrew Scriptures to initiate God's rule of righteousness. The "Christ" is seen by Christians as being Jesus of Nazareth.

---

* The definitions here relate to ways these terms are used in this study. Further explorations can be made in other resources, such as Donald K. McKim, *The Westminster Dictionary of Theological Terms,* 2nd ed. (Louisville, KY: Westminster John Knox Press, 2014).

Pharisees. Hebrew term meaning "separated ones." A Jewish party during the time of Jesus who obeyed the written law of Moses and its unwritten interpretations.

Sadducees. A priestly party during the time of Jesus who sought to preserve the identity, religion, and culture of the Jews.

scribes. Individuals who were trained to compose documents, often of a legal nature, and to serve as copyists, especially of the Hebrew Scriptures. They frequently became known as authorities in interpreting the Law and seem to have associated often with the Pharisees.

sin. Various biblical terms and themes refer to sin to express human separation from God because of opposition to God's purposes.

Torah. Hebrew term for "instruction," "law." God's revelation to Moses at Mt. Sinai expressed God's will in order to instruct the nation of Israel. The first five books of the Hebrew Scriptures (Old Testament) are known as the Torah.

Want to Know More?

Hare, Douglas R. A. *Matthew*. Interpretation: A Bible Commentary for Teaching and Preaching. Louisville, KY: John Knox Press, 1993.

Long, Thomas G. *Matthew*. Westminster Bible Companion. Louisville, KY: Westminster John Knox Press, 1997.

McKenzie, Alyce M. *Matthew*. Interpretation Bible Studies. Louisville, KY: Westminster John Knox Press, 1998.

Senior, Donald. *The Gospel of Matthew*. Interpreting Biblical Texts Series. Nashville, TN: Abingdon Press, 2011.

Wright, N. T. *Matthew for Everyone, Part 1: Chapters 1–15*. Louisville, KY: Westminster John Knox Press, 2004.

Wright, N. T. *Matthew for Everyone, Part 2: Chapters 16–28*. Louisville, KY: Westminster John Knox Press, 2011.

CPSIA information can be obtained
at www.ICGtesting.com
Printed in the USA
JSHW011952150820
7266JS00031B/214